LIFE SKILLS FOR TEENS

The ultimate guide for **Young Adults** on how to manage money, cook, clean, find a job, make better decisions, and everything you need to be independent.

Vivian Foster

SOMETHING FOR YOU!

Get your printable workbook today!

Scan this code to download.

Table of Contents

Introduction

"Education is the most powerful weapon which you can use to change the world."

–Nelson Mandela

So, your mom, aunt, or teacher put this book into your hands and there are about 99 things you'd rather be doing. Whether you're 13, 18, or 25, you may not be interested in picking up life lessons. After all, you have survived perfectly well until now, and it will probably be easy to do simple things like pay the rent, cook an omelet, or stick a pair of sneakers in the washing machine when you actually need to. In fact, just about the last thing you may feel like doing is learning how to iron a shirt, save cash, or solve problems.

On the other hand, you could be someone who wishes to take on more responsibility and learn skills that will make you more confident. These practical life lessons will serve you well into the future, so if you're keen to read on, more power to you!

When mom and dad start to nag you or your teachers start telling you how important it is to know how to sew, it may make you feel like "just another brick in the wall," as the song goes. I know how it feels because although I am a mom, it seems like yesterday that I was 17 and panicking about living at college for the first time. Moreover, I know teens pretty well because I have two teenage kids: My daughter Claire is 19, and my son Neil is 13.

I like to think I'm a pretty laid-back mom. I enjoy playing Minecraft and Fortnite with Neil, but I also know that there are many things I wish I had known when I was a teen. Claire had a pretty hard time when she first went to college. She barely knew how to cook or sew. I remember that once, she called me in hysterics when she found a pair of trousers she needed for a date and found the hem was broken. Claire also developed anxiety in her first year from the stress of exams and having to do everything herself.

I remember feeling very guilty that I had not taught Claire more life lessons before she left, and I started researching various subjects to help her when she came home for the summer. That first summer went by in a flash! We did quite a few things together, like learning a set number of healthy recipes she could then tweak and vary, sewing a few hems and buttons, and making DIY cleaning products.

Claire is now super excited about organizing her clothes and home. She actually enjoys organizing her wardrobe and shelves by color and making dinner for her college friends. She says she feels quite sophisticated when friends come home and comment on how beautifully designed and tidy her place is.

Your teen years will fly by, and you will probably recall them as the most wondrous years in your life. My aim in this book isn't to take up hours of your time, turn you into a "super kid" who would put Eleven in *Stranger Things* out of a job, or model you after Mr. Flanders from *The Simpsons*. Consider this a guidebook you can pick up when you need to know specific things. For instance, if a grandparent gives you a little money for college, what should you do with it? Should you just keep it in a piggy bank, deposit it in the bank (if you have an account), or invest it and make it double in size?

If you feel like you're just not good at numbers and savings, you are a lousy cook, or you could never change a tire if your life depended on it, think again. I am here to tell you all about the "growth mindset." This is the exact opposite of having a "fixed mindset." People with fixed mindsets think that they are born with (or without) fixed talents, skills, and abilities. Those with growth mindsets, on the other hand, know that the most valuable lessons in life can all be learned if you commit to them. Gordon Ramsay wasn't born making the juiciest roast on the planet. Coco Chanel did not grow up with fancy things. Marie Kondo (a whiz at tidying up with four million Instagram followers) had to learn the best way to organize clothing, books, and other items in her home by trial-and-error and by using her logic.

Now, here's the rub: Nobody's perfect. Marie Kondo may not be able to make a soufflé, but maybe Gordon Ramsay isn't an ace at folding shirts either. Throughout your life, you will continually pick up new skills. Your interests, strengths, and lifestyle will all determine what you are better at and what you need to improve upon.

When using this guide, you can simply jump straight to a chapter that interests you or read it from start to finish. I want you to know that if you feel a little insecure about some of your abilities, you are not alone! Let me share a few facts that will reveal that most teens can use a little help with practical skills like dressing up for a job interview, finding an apartment, or solving problems.[1]

---

[1] SWNS, 2021

Surprising Statistics:

- A recent survey has found that 81% of recent college graduates wish they had been taught more life skills before graduation.
- Around 30% of graduates don't have a good enough credit score to get a credit card, apply for a loan, or rent an apartment (28%).
- Around 43% cannot afford to pay for graduate school.
- The majority of young adults do not know how to invest, manage their student loans, or plan for their financial future.
- Three in ten feel bad about their lack of financial knowledge.
- One in five graduates do not know how to cook or do their own laundry.
- Some 26% do not know how to carry out basic maintenance tasks like unclogging a toilet or resetting a Wi-Fi router.
- Around 60% of millennials do not know how to make a simple salad dressing.
- More than a quarter of millennials do not know how to prepare a cake from a boxed mix.
- When shown a picture of a butter knife, only 63% of millennials knew what it was!

If you can relate to these statistics, don't feel bad. It's not the end of the world. Nothing bad will happen to you or your family if you burn an artichoke or walk around with a wrinkly shirt.

Things don't have to be so dramatic or black-or-white. You know how fabulous you feel when you're looking like a boss, your hair is styled well, and you've got cash to spend with friends at the mall or while out to lunch. Feeling on top of your "to-do" list, living in a tidy home, smelling nice, and having a part-time job can all help you feel more confident, independent, and "complete" when you first move away from home.

You should also know that there are many celebrities who are into budgeting, upcycling clothes, or starting a business. There are many examples in the celebrity world, including the following:

- Actress Jennie Garth teaches her kids to buy items they can mix and match so they learn not to overspend on fashion.
- Kristin Bell clips coupons to save money. Her kids learn that even though their parents are wealthy, they don't waste money or pass up a good bargain.
- Sarah Jessica Parker's children wear hand-me-downs.
- Euphoria's Sydney Sweeney started working on car maintenance when she was just a tot.
- Jamie Oliver's 11-year-old son has been cooking since he was a toddler. So has Gordon Ramsay's daughter, Tilly. She learned how to cook for one reason: to get her family's attention! By age 19, she already had her own cooking show.

Sometimes, adults like to portray teens as lazy or unmotivated, but these adjectives are actually unfounded. Many successful adults found their passion when they were your age or even younger.

Let's get to the nitty-gritty, then. This book will teach you practical life skills as well as useful emotional ones. I work as a teacher but have been an avid student of psychology for over 20 years. I know that when Claire went to college, some of her biggest problems were emotional ones—not getting enough sleep because of stress, feeling lonely and depressed, and feeling insecure about handling everyday responsibilities (like going to the doctor) for the first time without me.

I also remember her calling me for hour-long talks about conflicts with a roommate or classmate. In this book, I want to offer the advice I shared with her. Once Claire reached college-age, I was still her mom, but when I was teaching her practical or emotional skills, I tried to be more like her friend. I hope to do the same for you.

Claire and her friends say that my advice has helped them get through the typical challenges that arise in their daily life. And believe me, they faced many issues in their first year! The list of their "disasters" is large and sometimes a little comical. It includes the following anecdotes:

- The time Claire's cousin, Tim, started dating the girl of his dreams but couldn't afford to take her to a fancy restaurant.
  Solution: He learned to cook a few recipes of mine and made her a romantic dinner at home.
- Claire's classmate Megan woke up to find her electricity had been cut because she forgot to pay the bill.
  Solution: Megan now uses an app that reminds her when bills are due.
- Claire was offered various credit cards by the bank but didn't know which card to choose.
  Solution: By comparing interest rates, she was able to choose the card that cost her the least over the long run.
- Claire was offered an internship and didn't know what to wear to the office.
  Solution: She built a basic wardrobe with my help and now has at least one outfit for every important or professional event.

Once you leave home and start working, you will have to make a myriad of decisions. You will feel more adult than ever, yet sometimes, you'll wish you could curl up on the sofa back home with a big bowl of your favorite soup (Dad's special recipe)! If you have a supportive family, count on them for advice, information, and someone to listen.

Keep this book handy as well. I hope it will be a lifesaver for various needs and issues. By the time you have turned the last page, you will know how to:

- Stick to a budget, manage money, and make smart financial moves for your future.
- Prioritize a healthy diet and workout routine.
- Cook a delicious, nutritious, and impressive-looking meal.
- Manage your home.
- Look and feel good.
- Dress the part.
- Maintain your car in good working condition.
- Find your first rental apartment.
- Go to college and/or look for your first job.
- Overcome emotional challenges.
- Build healthy relationships with others.
- Reach for meaningful goals.
- Embrace healthy habits.
- Make good decisions.

You will learn many more skills, of course, so if you're curious to know what they are, read on!

Chapter One: Learning to Manage, Save, and Invest Money

"The more your money works for you, the less you have to work for money."

—*Idowu Koyenikan*

If words like *mortgage*, *interest rates*, or *credit score* confuse you, take heart. They confuse many of us adults as well! Let's take a look at a few statistics on financial literacy in the US:[2]

- Only 57% of American adults are financially literate. Being financially literate means knowing about finances, financial terms, obligations, and how to ensure one's future financial security.
- Typical families that file for bankruptcy owe more than 1.5 times their annual income in short-term, high-interest debt. A large portion of this is credit card debt.
- Being financially knowledgeable can make a big impact on your life. It will reduce your debt, improve your savings, and enable you to accumulate assets—homes, cars, and other items of value.[3]

---

[2] Milken Institute, 2021.
[3] Lonch, 2022.

The Importance of Financial Literacy

Lacking sound knowledge about finances can have major consequences for the rest of your life. Because of the high cost of college, many young people like yourself take out loans that take years to pay off.[4] Repaying these loans can make it hard to buy a house or enjoy a good quality of life when you are older, and it is important to know how to choose loans with the most favorable terms. By being financially savvy, you can avoid:

- vulnerability to frauds and scams
- inability to own a home or a car
- continual debt
- bankruptcy
- risky or damaging financial choices
- anxiety or depression from financial stress
- mortgages with high-interest rates

Important Financial Terms

As you delve deeper into financial topics, you will frequently come across specific terms. I will explain some of the most important ones below:

- **Interest:** This is the amount charged for borrowing money. For instance, if you borrow $100 from someone and the interest rate is 2% per year, the annual interest for that amount is $2, and by the end of the year, you will owe $102.
- **Compound Interest:** This is a bit harder to master, but it's all a matter of simple addition. Compounded interest involves making money from the interest you earn. In the above example, say you lent someone $100 at an

---

[4] Red Star Education, n.d.

interest rate of 2% per year. At the end of the year, they owe you $102. After the second year, they owe you 2% of $102, which means a total amount of $104.04. Interest can compound at different intervals (not only once a year). For this reason, it is much smarter to save your money in an account which pays compound interest.

- **Budget:** This is a list of all the things you must buy with the money you have. A typical budget includes rent, grocery bills, electricity, and water bills (unless the landlord pays for these), clothing, and a specific amount for leisure spending.

- **Savings Account:** You open a savings account in a bank to hold money for a long period of time. This is so you can save for larger goals such as a house or a car. The money grows interest in the bank, so the idea is to allow it to stay put unless you have an emergency.

- **Checking Account:** These accounts are for everyday use. They are designed to allow easy access to your cash. They often come with debit cards (which you can use to take out money or pay for things), checks (which you can write to pay someone money if you don't have cash on you), and digital payment options (like contactless payments via a smartphone app).

- **Debt:** This is a sum of money that is owed.

- **Inflation:** Did you ever hear your dad or mom say, "When I was a kid, you could buy a bar of chocolate for a quarter?" This is an example of inflation, which means the rate at which prices increase over a given time. Things sometimes get more expensive because there is a higher demand for products or services, and people are willing to pay more for them. Sometimes, governments impose taxes (added fees) on items you buy, which also increases their price.

- **Taxes:** You may have heard your parents talking about having to complete their tax returns or talking about how
- high taxes are. Taxes are the amount you pay the government for services that your country, state, or town needs. For example, the government needs these taxes for the military, roads, and schools.[5]
- **Net Pay:** This is the amount of money you actually take home after all payroll deductions are subtracted from your gross pay. For example, if you make $1,000 gross per month, and $150 is deducted for taxes and benefits, your net pay is $850.
- **Net Worth:** A person's net worth is the value of all their assets (money, cars, houses etc.) minus all their liabilities (in other words, minus the amounts they owe).

Fun Fact: The individuals with the highest net worth are Elon Musk (with a net worth of $219 billion) and Amazon's Jeff Bezos (whose net worth is $131.9 billion).

Money Fact: You must be at least 18 years old to open a bank account. However, if you are under this age, you can still open a joint account with a parent or legal guardian as the co-owner. Some banks have accounts specifically catered to minors so you can learn about banking as you go. By opening an account, you can earn interest on your savings!

---

[5] DMC, n.d.

Learning How to Budget

If you will soon be renting your first home or going off to college, you need to know how to create and follow a budget so you don't end up spending more than you have. To budget your spending, make sure to:

1. **Know the difference between needs and wants.** Needs include rent, groceries, clothing, and utilities. Wants are little luxuries like movie tickets, eating out, going to the gym, and going to concerts.
2. **Do a little math.** Subtract the total amount of needs from the amount you earn. This gives you how much money you have to "play around" with, as well as how much you need to save.
3. **Set aside money for savings** (I will explain more on this below).
4. **Look for ways to cut back on your spending if needed.** There are many apps that help you budget, discover what you are spending your money on, and help you identify areas of spending that need to be cut down. These include *Mint, Goodbudget, Toshl Finance*, and *Star Banks Adventure. Toshl Finance* targets your age group specifically (13 to 18), so you might want to start there. This app links to one or more real bank accounts, and it provides you with charts and visualizations that depict your spending patterns. It's a magnificent way to discover the hidden ways you might be wasting money that could be employed more wisely or set aside for your savings goals.[6]

---

[6] Atlanta Parent, 2021.

Learning How to Save

How much should you save per month? Aim to have at least three times your monthly expenses in your savings account. Why so much? Well, if an emergency occurs (for instance, your pet needs emergency surgery, you lose a tooth and need treatment, or you get a job and need to buy an electric scooter to get there), savings come in handy.

How Much Should You Save?

If you have a part-time job, try to set aside around 10% of what you earn per month.[7] Financial advisors usually advise that adults set aside 20% of their salary. However, this amount may vary depending on the stage of life, and some financial advisors recommend that you should only save around 10% of your salary or monthly allowance if you are under 25 years old.

---

[7] Consumer Financial Protection Bureau, n.d.

Savings Tips

Just a few ways to cut down on your monthly
expenditure include:

- **Cook most meals at home.** A dish that costs you
  $20 in a restaurant or via home delivery may cost
  as little as $4.50 if you prepare it yourself. There
  are so many cool ways to find recipes that you
  can make in under 15 minutes. Check out Jamie
  Oliver, BBC Good Food's Recipes for Teenagers,
  and even TikTok for fun, healthy, easy, and
  affordable recipes.
- **Live in a shared apartment.** If you live with
  roommates, your rental costs will drop
  considerably. Ideally, you should move in with
  people you know and trust. You can also check
  out notice boards at your college, which usually
  have ads for shared rental accommodations. If
  you move in with people you don't know, make
  it a point to socialize with them a couple of times
  beforehand to ensure you are on the same
  wavelength. Pay a visit to the apartment to see if
  they keep it clean and tidy.
- **Shop for clothes in vintage shops.** By buying
  second-hand items, you can not only make
  significant savings but also find cool designer
  clothing and accessories. You can also do your
  share to help fight global warming. Many clothes
  are discarded without being worn, and landfills
  across the globe are already stuffed to the brim.
- **Buy second-hand books.** College books can be
  very costly, so you should always try to rent or
  buy used books.

Check out AbeBooks, CampusBooks, and CollegeBooksDirect. Search on college forums and social media, in case students are selling books in your local area or faculty.

- **Have home movie nights and dinner parties.** This will reduce your total leisure spending.

Taking Your First Steps in Investment

Investing is a great way to learn how you can "make money from money." It involves buying an asset (a type of property) with the expectation that its value will go up. Typical assets people invest in include:

- **Stocks:** Consider an investment in stocks as equivalent to buying a small part of a company. Stocks are bought and sold on a stock exchange through a broker.
- **Bonds:** These are loans you can invest in through a bond trust that is traded on the stock exchange.
- **Real Estate:** This type of property includes houses, land, apartments, and similar. You may not be able to own a whole house yet, but you can invest in real estate through a trust on the stock exchange.

You have to be an adult to buy stocks by yourself, but with the help of your parents, you can still invest. To do so, you would need to open a "joint brokerage account" through an investing app for beginners. These are like typical accounts, but they can have two or more authorized owners.

Useful Terms for New Investors

In addition to knowing a bit about interest and compound interest, it is also important to know the meaning of the following terms:

- **Diversification:** People who regularly invest usually do so in diverse (various) options, including stocks, cash, real estate, commodities, bonds, and more.[8] This is a way to avoid "putting all your eggs into one basket." If you lose money from one investment, you still have the chance to make money from another one.

- **Risk Tolerance:** This refers to the size of risk you are willing to take to earn a profit from your investments. Some investments are high-risk, but they have the potential to make you a lot of money (and, potentially, suffer big losses). Other investments are safer, but the profits you earn may be less.[9]

- **Mutual Funds:** A mutual fund is a company that pools money from various investors and invests the money in securities such as stocks, bonds, and short-term debt.[10] When you invest in a mutual fund, you can potentially own part of thousands of companies. The specific investments are chosen by an investment manager.

- **Index Funds:** Experts often advise new investors to try index funds. These funds invest in a specific list of securities such as stocks on popular indexes such as S&P 500, NASDAQ, and Dow Jones. An index fund is a type of mutual fund or exchange-traded

---

[8] Freedom Sprout, n.d.
[9] Minyanville, 2021.
[10] U.S. Securities and Education Commission, n.d.

fund with a portfolio that tracks a financial market index.[11]

- **Exchange-Traded Funds (ETFS):** These funds trade on exchanges just like stocks, so their prices change throughout the day. Mutual funds, on the other hand, only change their prices once a day—after the close of regular trading hours.
- **The Rule of 72:** This is a handy rule to know if you want to calculate how many years it will take your investment to double in size. You simply divide the number 72 by the annual interest rate to find how many years you will have to wait. For instance, if the annual interest rate is 3%, it will take 24 years for your investment to double.[12]

Before Investing

Start by opening a checking and/or savings account so you learn how to use ATMs, stay within your daily transaction limits, and control how money goes in and out of your bank. You can then diversify by investing in individual stocks, mutual funds, and exchange-traded funds.

Utilizing Helpful Apps

Cool investment apps and accounts for beginners include:

- *Greenlight*: This app has no trading fees and allows you to buy fractional shares from your favorite companies. It also has education

---

[11] Fernando, 2020.
[12] Freedom Sprout, n.d.

features that teach you about ideas like compound growth.[13]

- **_Fidelity Youth Account_**: This is a teen-owned brokerage account you can use if your parents have a Fidelity account. It allows you to spend, save, and invest with one handy tool, and you can start investing by buying fractional shares for a minimum of $1.
- **_Stockpile_**: This app is free, and although it requires parental supervision, it allows you to choose the stocks you wish to buy and sell.

Knowing the Difference Between Good and Bad Debt

Good debt is an investment; it helps you increase your net worth or enhance your life in an important way. Bad debt involves borrowing money to purchase items whose value drops quickly or to buy something you enjoy. Examples of good debts are those used for education, your own business, or real estate. Examples of bad debts include those used to buy cars (which depreciate quickly), designer clothes, and furniture. Of course, you may need to buy these items for your work and/or daily life, but you should avoid using credit cards with high-interest rates to do so.

Building a Good Credit Score

When you ask for a loan, your banks look at your credit score. Consider this a way for the bank to assess if you are a "good bet." Having a good credit score lets a bank know that you will pay them back without a problem. A credit score has three digits and generally ranges from 300 to 850. Generally, a score of around 670 to 739 is considered good, 740 to 799 is very good,

---

[13] Berger, 2022.

and 800+ is excellent.[14] Some ways to build your credit include doing the following:

- **Study various options carefully when shopping for a credit card.** Look into features such as the annual percentage rate, additional fees, fraud protection, automated payment reminders, foreign transaction fees, and rewards. If you have more than one credit card, avoid using the one that charges a higher interest rate.
- **Pay your debts on time.** This will show you are a trustworthy payer.
- **Review your credit report once a year.**[15] You can ask for a free copy of your credit report from each of three major credit reporting agencies—Equifax®, Experian®, and TransUnion®—once a year at AnnualCreditReport.com or call toll-free Tel: 1-877-322-8228. Doing so will enable you to see if anyone is claiming that you owe them money. It will also give you the chance to correct any errors you find.
- **Aim to use 30% credit or less so that you have a good credit utilization ratio.** Show that you are capable of living with what you have and that you don't need to borrow too much to cover your needs.
- **Fatten up your credit score with services like *Rental Kharma* or *RentTrack*.** If you pay rent every month, services like *Rental Kharma* and *RentTrack* will report your rent payments to the credit bureaus on your behalf, which in turn could help raise your credit score.

---

[14] Equifax, n.d.
[15] Wells Fargo, n.d.

Test time!

It is time to complete a quick test on the information I shared with you. Check your answers at the end of the chapter:

1. What is a credit score?
   a. A three-digit number that lets financial institutions know if you are a good bet for a loan
   b. The interest rate of your credit card
   c. A score that says how much credit you have used
2. What is debt?
   a. Money you spend
   b. Money earned from business activities
   c. An amount owed
3. What is interest?
   a. The original amount you borrowed
   b. The amount charged for borrowing money
   c. The profit you make when you sell something
4. What is a checking account for?
   a. Your daily needs
   b. Your savings
   c. Investment
5. What is risk tolerance?
   a. The amount you are willing to risk when you make an investment
   b. The amount of profit you can make from an investment
   c. An aggressive means of investing

Now that your money issues are under control, you can concentrate on learning to lead a healthy lifestyle (whether you are still living with your parents, or you have moved to a new rental home). Doing so will not only help you look fit and buff, but also make you happier. In the next chapter, you will learn about the incredible link between your gut and your mind and many more fascinating topics!

Test Answers:
1. a
2. c
3. b
4. a
5. a

Chapter Two: Boosting Your Physical and Mental Health

"All progress takes place outside the comfort zone."

–Michal Joan Bobak

When you're in the middle of a game of *Fortnite* and you and your buddies are defending yourselves against other teams online, it may be really hard to end the game and head outside for an outdoor workout. If you neglect your physical needs, however, you may find that your focus suffers, you start to feel a bit down in the dumps, and you don't feel as energetic as you once did. In this chapter, I will explain why prioritizing your physical and mental health is essential from the time you are young.

Facts About Teen Health in the US

- About 14.7 million children and adolescents in the US are obese. Fast food, an indoor lifestyle, and an excessive reliance on technology for entertainment are all to blame;[16] though other factors can also be at play.
- Allowing yourself to gain a lot of weight can affect many more things than your jeans size. It can damage your self-confidence and stop you from taking part in activities that require you to be in good shape. It is also linked to a higher likelihood of developing depression.[17]

---

[16] Centers for Disease Control and Prevention, n.d.
[17] Villagrasa Blasco et al., 2020

- Being inactive can lead to a host of diseases, including type 2 diabetes and heart disease. Enjoying a healthy diet and exercising regularly can prevent these diseases. It can also increase your ability to battle stress.[18]

The Six Pillars of Health and Wellness for Teens

Consider the road to health and wellness as one built on six pillars: a healthy diet, regular exercise, good sleep, responsible social media use, positive hobbies, and a daily hygiene routine.

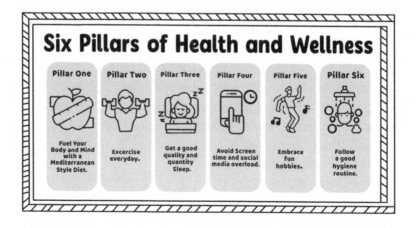

Pillar One: Fuel Your Body and Mind With a Mediterranean-Style Diet

You don't have to follow a strict diet to have all the fuel you need to think clearly, concentrate at school or work, or stay at a healthy weight. Doctors generally recommend that people without special dietary needs follow a Mediterranean diet. This super-easy eating plan includes lean meat, plenty of fruit and vegetables, grains, legumes, and healthy fats sourced from fatty fish (like wild salmon and tuna) and extra-virgin olive oil. Healthy

[18] John Hopkins Medicine, n.d.

fats contain Omega-3 essential fatty acids, which are good for the brain and the heart.[19]

A general guideline for the Mediterranean diet is as follows:

- Build your meals around vegetables, beans, and whole grains.
- Consume fish twice a week.
- Cook and dress foods with healthy fats.
- Enjoy fresh fruit for dessert.

Instead of obsessing over calories and carbohydrates, follow this simple plan:

- About half of your plate should contain fruits and vegetables.
- Combine produce with whole grains like whole-wheat bread, brown rice, and whole-grain cereal. Avoid refined cereals and sweets, white bread, and white rice.
- Choose lean meats like turkey, chicken, or fish. Alternatively, use plant-based protein sources like beans, nuts, tofu, eggs, and seafood.
- Drink fat-free or low-fat milk to build healthy muscles and bones. The US Department of Agriculture recommends that teens consume at least three glasses of milk (or dairy equivalents) per day.

If you find it hard to calculate the amounts of fruits and vegetables you should be eating, just use cup measurements. Aim to eat between one-and-a-half and two cups of fruit a day and between two-and-a-half and three cups of vegetables per

---

[19] Mayo Clinic, n.d.

day. Note that two cups of leafy greens (like kale or spinach) count as a single cup serving.

Another easy tip to follow is to chomp on fruits and vegetables of different colors (think red and green peppers, carrots, apples, beetroots, and oranges) because all these foods have different nutrients. You can spread these portions throughout your day between your three main meals and snacks.

Don't forget legumes like lentils, chickpeas, and black-eyed peas. These are very easy to cook and taste wonderful—especially in a stew or soup in the winter! If you like hummus, make some at home with canned chickpeas. It will take less than five minutes to do so. Just blend a can of chickpeas with garlic, salt, olive oil, tahini, and fresh lemon juice to taste, and you will have a lovely snack to enjoy with pita bread or freshly sliced vegetables like celery or carrots.

Make a weekly meal plan and go to the supermarket once or twice a week so you don't end up shopping at the last minute. When you're stressed, hungry, or pressed for time, it is easy to give into cravings for refined, sugary, and salty foods.

Fun Fact: "You are what you eat" is an old saying, but it is certainly true when it comes to the gut-brain connection. This connection can be strengthened by ensuring you have a wide array of healthy bacteria in your gut. Can bacteria be healthy? Indeed, it can! Not all bacteria are gross or disease-producing. Some are like "superheroes" that fight off bad bacteria, restore balance to the body, and help you feel better. Studies indicate that having low levels of some types of gut bacteria is linked to depression.[20] To build a healthy habitat for gut bacteria, eat lots of fiber (including vegetables, chickpeas, berries, and whole wheat pasta). You can also feed these life-sustaining microorganisms with probiotic foods like tempeh, kimchi, kefir, yogurt, pickles, and sauerkraut.

Pillar Two: Exercise Every Day

The US Department of Health and Human Services recommends that adolescents enjoy an hour or more of moderate-to-vigorous exercise daily. As part of your routine, you should include muscle-strengthening exercises at least three days a week and bone-strengthening activities at least three days a week.[21]

Your exercise routine should include:

- **Cardiovascular Exercise:** This type of activity keeps your heart and respiratory system in good shape. It can

---

20 VIB, 2019.
21 Centers for Disease Control and Prevention, n.d.

include running, jumping rope, cycling, swimming, and vigorous dancing.

If you can, wear a Fitbit or other fitness watch to make sure you are within your target heart rate. Your target heart rate sits at between 50% and 85% of your maximum heart rate.

Your maximum heart rate depends on your age. To calculate your target heart rate, use a free online calculator like the Target Heart Rate Calculator on Active.com. You simply need to indicate your age and the appropriate percentage of your maximum heart rate, and press calculate. You will find that if you are aged 13, your target heart rate is somewhere between 176 and 203 beats. If you are 19, your target heart rate is between 171 and 200 beats.[22]

- **Muscle-Strengthening Exercises:** These can include push-ups, sit-ups, and squats. You can also use light free weights or resistance bands. If you want to work out with weights for the first time, you should do so under the guiding hand of a professional (like a personal trainer, coach, or teacher). They will ensure you perform all exercises with the right technique. You can start with one or two sets of eight to 12 repetitions and gradually increase these numbers.

- **Bone-Strengthening Exercises:** Boost your bone strength by climbing steps, playing tennis, dancing, jogging, hiking, and doing weights.[23]

---

[22] Live Strong, n.d.
[23] Kids Health, n.d.

- **Stress-Busting activities:** If you feel stressed out by exams or by having to juggle so many activities, know that there are powerful ways to lower your stress levels and enjoy greater focus and a better mood. If you're into science, check out the numerous studies proving that holistic activities like yoga, controlled breathing, and Tai Chi all lower levels of stress hormones and stop panic attacks in their tracks.

  Apps like *Calm* and *Headspace* will guide you through a host of exercises to help you meditate, sleep, or calm down in the lead-up to stressful events like exams.

  Finally, try to spend at least 10 minutes in a green area (a park, the woods, or the seashore). Simply being in a majestic green or blue spot for a few minutes significantly lowers levels of the stress hormone, cortisol.[24]

Pillar Three: Get Good Quantity and Quality Sleep

Getting a good night's sleep does more than help you stay awake during class. This requires getting enough sleep, but not just any sleep; it must be good quality as well. In other words, both quantity and quality matter. The American Academy of Sleep Medicine recommends that teens aged 13 to 18 obtain eight to 10 hours of sleep every night.[25]

When sleep quantity or quality are lacking, you can:

- Find it hard to concentrate.
- Get poor grades.

---

[24] Meredith et al., 2020
[25] Centers for Disease Control and Prevention, n.d.

- Become involved in drowsy driving incidents.
- Increase your risk of anxiety and depression.
- Be more irritable with others.
- Have headaches and migraines.
- Put on weight.
- Feel dizzy.

> **Not-So-Fun Fact:** A lack of sleep can lead to weight gain because it is linked to growth hormone deficiency and elevated cortisol levels, both of which are related to obesity.

What Is Good Quality Sleep?

You are achieving your sleep quality goals if:[26]

- You regularly wake up no more than once a night.
- It takes you half an hour or less to fall asleep when you get into bed.
- You fall back asleep within twenty minutes if you wake up in the middle of the night.
- You feel re-energized (not tired or fatigued) when you wake up in the morning.
- You don't crave junk food during the day to get you out of a slump.
- You don't feel more stressed out or angrier than usual.

The Six Steps to a Good Night's Sleep

If you feel tired during the day and alert at night, you wake up frequently during the night, or you find it hard to fall asleep when you get into bed, your routine could use a change. Follow my six-step routine, and you will enjoy a good rest every night.

---

[26] Sleep Foundation, 2022.

1. **Keep it dark and quiet.** Your bedroom should be completely dark and soundproof since light and sounds will keep you alert or awake. Use blackout curtains and make sure all your windows are well-sealed.
2. **Cool it down.** The temperature for optimal sleep is between 60- and 67-degrees Fahrenheit. Why so cool? Because your body is programmed to experience a slight temperature drop in the evening. By turning the temperature down, you help regulate your body temperature and let it know it's time for sleep.
3. **Avoid caffeine, tea, cola beverages, and any other drinks that can make you feel wakeful from about mid-afternoon onward.** Avoid large meals before bedtime as well.
4. **Avoid screen use in the afternoon/evening if you can, as the light screens emit can keep you alert.** Shut down all screens as a matter of habit at least one hour before you intend to sleep. If you are bored, read a book instead.
5. **Consider playing some white noise.** Some people find this drowns out environmental noise and helps them fall asleep.
6. **Establish a routine and stick to it every night.** Try to avoid the temptation of staying up until 1 am or 2 am chatting with a friend.

> **Not-So-Fun Fact:** Teens are biologically predisposed to a later sleep time because their natural sleep-wake cycle changes as they age[27]. It is hard to fight the natural tendency to sleep later, but you can do so with a sound sleep strategy.

Smart Tip: If you want to feel extra alert, step outside into the sun in the morning for fifteen to thirty minutes. This will help reset your circadian rhythm.

Pillar Four: Avoid Screen Time and Social Media Overload

Recent Pew Research indicates that 95% of teens have access to a smartphone,[28] and around 45% of adolescents admit to being online almost constantly. Too much screen time can interfere with your school, social life, health, and wellbeing in many ways.[29] Just a few consequences it can have are as follows:

- poor sleep quantity and quality
- increased risk of obesity
- loss of cognitive ability (your ability to reason, problem-solve, understand complex ideas, and learn)
- increased aggression
- desensitization to violent content
- lower self-esteem
- higher stress levels

---

[27] Duffy, 2019.
28 Anderson & Jiang, 2018.
29 Active Health, n.d.

Social Media Overload

Social media use is also linked to mental health issues, like depression and anxiety. A 2019 study on over 12,000 teens found that using social media sites and apps over three times a day predicts poor mental health and well-being in teens.[30]

Making the Most of Social Media

Social media can have many benefits. It enables you to communicate with friends, helps you create fun online identities, and allows you to be part of active networks with shared interests. It can also teach you about appropriate behavior and humor, and some sources can present current events and facts dynamically.

To get the most out of social media, don't stop using it altogether; try to set reasonable limits for social media interaction, enjoy more face-to-face time with friends, and avoid gossiping online. Make sure to report any instances of cyberbullying to your parents and/or teachers.

> **Not-So Fun Facts:** You may wonder how screen time can affect your ability to learn. It is simple: It alters the structure of your brain, causing gray matter (which is responsible for cognitive processes) to shrink. In very young children, it causes white matter (which plays a role in the brain's signal communication system) to lose its structural integrity.[31] Studies on teens have shown that internet-addicted boys have reduced cortical thickness in the frontal lobe. This is the part of the brain responsible for planning, organization, self-

30 Mayo Clinic, n.d.
31 Hutton et al., 2019.

> monitoring, and controlling your responses in order to achieve a goal.

Too much time spent on activities like gaming can also make your brain crave these experiences in the same way that a person with addiction may crave drugs. This is because too much gaming can affect your brain's reward system.

Studies also show that screen time can damage the insula—a part of the brain that is involved in our capacity to develop empathy and compassion for other human beings.[32]

A Fascinating Study: Research has shown that children who have limited screen time sleep better, perform better at school, exhibit better behavior, and have a reduced risk of unhealthy weight gain.[33] Lowering exposure to violent media, in particular, increases positive social interaction and decreases aggression.

What Can You Do to Reduce Your Screen Time?

To reduce your screen use in a way that doesn't seem like punishment, fill your life with fun activities! These can range from sports to camping, going on a road trip with your family, learning a new skill (like scuba diving or drawing), and indeed any activity that you enjoy. Additional tips include:

- Agreeing on a reasonable schedule for screen time with your parents. The 24-Hour Movement Guidelines indicate teens should only get two hours of recreational screen time a day.[34] Currently, teens spend an average of around eight hours in front of a screen daily.[35]

---

32 Perina, 2014.
33 Iowa State University, 2014.
34 Participation, 2018.
35 Catana, 2022.

- Agreeing to avoid screens during mealtimes and other family bonding times.
- Celebrating Screen-free Sunday (or indeed any other day of the week, in the same way that some people celebrate meat-free Mondays).

Pillar Five: Embrace Fun Hobbies

People who engage in their favorite hobbies regularly are less likely to experience stress, low mood, and depression. Group activities like team sports can be particularly beneficial when it comes to creating supportive relationships.

Art, music, and pursuits like theater and dance, meanwhile, enhance your creativity, happiness, and spiritual and emotional growth.

Making the most of leisure time spent on hobbies is simple: do something you are skilled at that you also happen to love. Don't take part in activities because you should or because everyone else is into them. Choose hobbies that fulfil your passions.

Pillar Six: Follow a Hygiene Routine

In order to present your best self to others, it is important to shower daily and wash your hair every two to three days. You can even add pampering products (such as body and facial scrubs) to your routine to make it more motivating. Keep skin in good condition by applying moisturizer after you bathe or shower.

Your appearance affects your self-confidence and the way you interact with others. Aim to look your best and take time to style your hair with a hair dryer or other equipment. If you have curly hair, moisture is extra-important. Invest in a good leave-on conditioner or use natural ingredients like coconut oil to seal in moisture.

Make sure your nails are clean and well-groomed. File them so they don't get caught on fabric or tear. If your nails are brittle or fragile, use a nail hardener and top it up with a clear topcoat, which can be natural or shiny. If you are into color, you can buy beautiful accessories and create beautiful designs at home. For a long-lasting manicure or pedicure, try gel or acrylic nails. These have to be applied by a professional but if you want to save money, you can do a course and learn how to create dazzling nail work yourself.

Most teens have normal-to-oily skin. It is essential to follow a daily routine that includes cleansing your skin well, toning it, and applying a moisturizer. Many people think that if they have oily skin, they should avoid moisturizers, but the opposite is actually true! When your skin is dry, your oil glands can go into overdrive, and the result is too much oil and the appearance of blackheads and other pore-related problems. If you have acne, you should see a dermatologist, who can recommend a good treatment. Most acne treatments contain ingredients like salicylic acid, which helps prevent the appearance of pimples.

A True Story: When Claire gets stressed out, she regularly goes into the forest and has a "forest bath." Her Japanese friend, Himari, told her that this hobby was big in Japan (where it is called shinrin-yoku). Forest bathing involves visiting a green area and opening all your senses (the senses of sound, sight, and touch, in particular) to the majesty of your surroundings. This habit has a powerful ability to restore your peace and calm and make you happier.

Test time!

1. How many hours should teens ideally spend on screens every day?
   a. Eight hours
   b. Two hours
   c. Five hours
2. What is the ideal temperature for a bedroom at bedtime?
   a. Between 60- and 67-degrees Fahrenheit
   b. Between 60 and 67 degrees Celsius
   c. 75- and 80-degrees Fahrenheit
3. What is shinrin-yoku?
   a. A type of dance
   b. Spending time in a forest and opening your senses to everything around you
   c. A healthy dish
4. What oil or fat is healthiest?
   a. Sunflower oil
   b. Butter
   c. Extra-virgin olive oil
5. How often should you eat fish a week?
   a. At least twice a week
   b. Once a month
   c. Every day

Now that you know how to stay healthy and take care of your appearance, it's time to forge ahead and learn how to manage medical matters when you move out of home.

Test Answers:
1. b
2. a
3. b
4. c
5. a

Chapter Three: Managing Medical Matters

"The greatest wealth is health."

–Virgil

When you live at home, your parents usually take care of contacting the doctor, buying your medications, and helping you heal from small issues like sunburn, cuts, and the flu. It can be a bit of a shock when you realize that you are suddenly in charge of your own health, but this responsibility isn't as difficult to manage as it may seem, so long as you are organized. In this chapter, you will learn how to contact your doctor, fill a prescription, and know what services are covered by health insurance.

Moving Away Can Be Stressful

Moving away to attend college can be tense. College students oftentimes find themselves more prone to catching colds and flu, due to factors such as:

- stress
- lack of sleep
- new environments
- dorms with poor hygiene conditions
- failure to prepare healthy meals and stay active

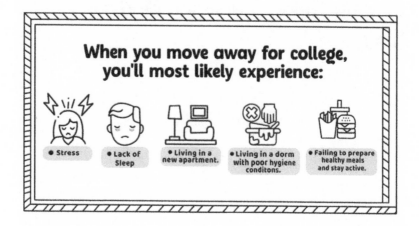

When you move away for college, you'll most likely experience:

- Stress
- Lack of Sleep
- Living in a new apartment.
- Living in a dorm with poor hygiene conditons.
- Failing to prepare healthy meals and stay active.

If you have signs of a bacterial infection, high fever, or an illness that lasts longer than a few days, you should see your doctor. Even if you just feel that something is not quite right with your health, it is a good idea to seek professional advice. Read on to discover ways to make the process smoother.

Discovering Campus Resources

During college orientation, students are taught about the resources that are available to them. Pay particular attention to health resources. Some colleges have full-service clinics on campus, while others have ties to local providers. Your college may also have affiliated urgent care centers nearby, which can come in handy if you suddenly feel ill.

Relying on Online Resources

It can be hard to decide whether you need to see a doctor or when a health matter is an emergency. Check out resources like:
- The American College Health Association's index (searching for "College Health Topics" on ACHA.org)
- Family Doctor (Familydoctor.org)

The topics covered on these sites are numerous. They include anxiety, mono, mumps, substance abuse, and tobacco use, though they have information on practically all pertinent health issues.

Why Do College Students Visit the Doctor?

Some of the most common reasons why college students visit medical professionals include:[36]

- urinary tract infections
- strep throat
- pneumonia
- mono
- the flu
- upper respiratory infections
- stomach bugs

Prevention Is Better Than Cure

Because you may be living far from your family during your college years or when you first move away of home, keeping illness at bay is important. In Chapter Two, I mentioned healthy habits you should adopt (such as consuming a healthy diet, getting a good night's sleep, and exercising regularly). You can also opt to have recommended vaccinations for people your age. Finally, maintain good hygiene by washing your hands frequently and keeping a clean, sanitized kitchen.

Compiling Your Medical History

Before leaving home, compile copies of medical records like dental x-ray films, blood work results, and similar. If you are 18,

---

36 Care Spot, n.d.

you can ask your health professionals to provide you with a copy or send your records to a new provider. If you are under 18, a parent or guardian may have to accompany you to ask for these documents.[37] Make sure to ask for these records in due time. Your health care provider has up to thirty days to provide them (though most do so more quickly than this).

Your records should include information such as the date of your last physical exam, past tests or screenings, your blood type, allergy information, a list of medications you are taking, and information on how long you have been doing so.

Top Tip: Ask your parents about their medical history as well in case future health professionals ask you for the information.

Finding a New Doctor

Before leaving home, visit your usual doctor and get a recommendation. They may know one or more excellent medical professionals in the city or area you will be moving to. You can also ask friends and family for recommendations. It always pays to visit a doctor that your loved ones say is trustworthy, caring, and efficient.

You will need to ensure that your new doctor is considered "in-network" or covered by your insurance plan. Some insurance companies have a "find a doctor" search button on their websites, but if yours does not, you can always use the

---

37 Teens Health, n.d.

American Medical Association's *DoctorFinder* tool. Just enter the appropriate zip code and the specialty you require.

Are You Covered by Your Parents' Health Insurance?

Until you are 26 years old, you can remain on your parents' insurance plan. This is the case even if you have a job or get married. If you are not covered, you can take out a short-term policy between college and when you are employed. Once you are employed, you will usually be covered by an employer plan. This involves your employer paying part of your health coverage.

If you are under 19, uninsured, and your family's income is below a certain level, you might be entitled to state help via the State Children's Health Insurance Program. For further information, contact your state's Department of Health and Human Services. Another option to check if you earn a low income or have a disability is Medicaid. Discover more by researching your state's Department of Health and Human Development (HHD) program.[38]

Filling and Refilling a Prescription

When you hear the phrase "filling a prescription," it almost sounds as if you have to fill out a form. In fact, this term simply describes the action the pharmacist undertakes when they put the right dosage into a bottle. Even if you haven't passed by and picked up the pills yet, once the medication is in the bottle, the prescription is considered "filled."

Getting a prescription filled essentially involves seeing your health provider, who will either write a paper script you can

---

38 Teens Health, n.d.

present to a local pharmacy or call a specific pharmacy to order the medication. Your provider may also send your prescription to the pharmacy via computer linked to their electronic medical record (EMR).

It is a good idea to buy your medications from the same pharmacy as much as possible, so they know you and have a record of any other medications you are taking. Some medications interact poorly with others, so you should always inform your health provider regarding any other medication you are taking and do online research on possible interactions.

To refill your prescriptions, follow the same plan. There are many apps that will remind you that your medications are due to run out soon. Check out apps like *Time Tune*, *RunMyLife*, and *Wunderlist*. You can also use *Google Calendar* to track pending tasks and appointments.

Some medications are covered by your health plan, while others are not. Some medications are partially covered, meaning you must pay part of their cost. This is called a "co-pay."

A True Story: My daughter, Claire, had always been very attached to our family doctor, Wendy. Claire was scared that she wouldn't have the same trust with her new doctor and that nobody else would treat her with the same care and friendship. However, Dr. Wendy recommended someone she had studied with in college: Dr. Gosling. Claire discovered that she had so much in common with her new doctor, including an interest in yoga and essential oils. Today, Claire considers Dr. Gosling her "health guru."

Test time!

1. Why do college students catch colds easily?
   a. Stress
   b. A lack of sleep
   c. Both of the above and more reasons
2. How long can a medical professional take to provide you with your personal medical records?
   a. Twenty days
   b. Forty days
   c. Thirty days
3. Until what age can you remain on your parents' insurance plan?
   a. 24
   b. 26
   c. 19
4. Who actually "fills" a prescription?
   a. The doctor
   b. You
   c. The pharmacist
5. What tool can help you find a doctor who is covered by your insurance plan?
   a. DoctorFinder
   b. DoctorNurse
   c. FindYourDoctor

It can be very hard to keep your health in good check if you are constantly eating fast foods. By learning to cook, you can reduce your food spending while consuming all the nutrients your body needs to function at its best. In Chapter Four, I will provide you with a host of handy tips on how to shop for food and cook a few delicious, nutritious recipes.

Test Answers:

1. c
2. c
3. b
4. c
5. a

Chapter Four: Learning to Cook Healthy Meals

"Your diet is a bank account. Good food choices are good investments."

–Bethenny Frankel

When I was at school, we used to have cooking classes, and our teacher once asked each of us to bring ingredients to cook a dish. I remember my mom taught me how to make an easy chicken curry. At the time, I remember I found it hard because there were quite a few ingredients to chop and slice. However, my dish was a big success among my classmates, and to this day, I cook that exact recipe for my family, always remembering my mom when I do so. Mom took plenty of time to teach us to make everything from homemade pancakes to spaghetti. I'm really thankful she did because back then, there was no Internet, and if you wanted to learn how to cook, you had to read cookbooks or ask someone to teach you.

Today, teens are so lucky. TikTok is especially great when it comes to quick, creative recipes. I use TikTok myself and have made quite a few fun recipes from this app with my son, including oven-baked chicken tenders covered in crispy cornflakes and homemade nuggets rolled in Takis. When you try cooking for the first time, find recipes that inspire you to be your most creative self.

Cooking Is Just Another Hobby, and It's Fun!

A recent study by Lancaster University researchers[39] shows that young people lack confidence and skills in the kitchen and that they consider sticking a pizza in the microwave to be cooking. Bear in mind that frozen, store-bought pizza has very little nutritional value and lots of preservatives and refined ingredients, which can promote weight gain and diabetes. One thing that fast food fans often ignore is that refined foods don't taste that great. To appreciate the difference, however, you have to experience dishes that are made from scratch with quality ingredients.

Buying Healthy Produce

Ask any top chef, and they will tell you that quality is everything when it comes to cooking. It's very difficult to go wrong when you have fresh, seasonal, and organic ingredients (including good cuts of meat if you are an omnivore) to work with. Try to visit a local farm and see how produce is grown. If you have a garden, grow simple vegetables and fruits like cabbages, tomatoes, chili, and herbs. Even if you don't have an outdoor space, you can grow sprouts in just three days in your kitchen. There is something about growing your own food that makes it more exciting to prepare and eat. It also gives you the experience you need to identify produce when it is at its best and to appreciate the wonder of fresh textures and flavors.

Making Organic Produce a Priority

When shopping for produce like fruits and vegetables from a farmer's market, farm, or supermarket, try to buy organic foods if you can. Unfortunately, these are more costly (typically between 10% and 20% more expensive) than conventionally

---

39 Tyrell et al., 2015.

grown produce. You may have to wait until you are working to afford them, but knowing their benefits is useful for the future.

The reason many dietitians recommend organic produce is because it has more antioxidants than conventionally grown produce.[40] A diet that is high in antioxidants can help reduce the risk of many diseases (including heart disease and some types of cancer).

> **Fun Fact:** Antioxidants function like a little army that fights free radicals. The latter damage cells and make you look and feel older than your biological age. By consuming a diet that is high in antioxidant goodness, you give your body a chance to fight aging and your skin, hair, and nails will be all the more beautiful for it.

Buy Fruits and Vegetables of Various Colors

Different colors indicate different types of nutritional content in produce. For instance, orange vegetables are high in beta-carotene, which boosts your eye health, while green, leafy vegetables contain lutein and zeaxanthin, as well as folate, vitamins, and antioxidants (which boost brain development). Bag fruits and vegetables separately from each other and separately from meat and seafood.[41] The raw juices from meat and seafood can contain harmful bacteria that make you ill.

Fun Fact: If you're wondering why fruit and vegetables shouldn't be bagged or stored together, here's the answer. Some fruits emit a gas called ethylene glycol, which quickens ripening and

40 Vallverdú-Queralt et al., 2012.
41 Healthy Options, 2018.

can cause some vegetables to spoil. Some fruits also absorb odors from vegetables, which reduces their appeal.

Tips for Buying Meat Products

When buying meat, choose products that have not been pre-seasoned or processed to ensure it is fresh and ready to use in your chosen recipes. Have a look at the meat in the tray or in the butcher's shop and make sure it is free of bruises, discoloration, and any signs that it may be poor quality or old. The surface of the meat should not be too dry, wet, or have any strange fluids. If you are buying beef, make sure the color is bright red (not brown, gray, or greenish).

If when you open your purchased meat, it smells rancid, avoid it. When you poke meat, it should go back to its original shape after a few seconds. If the indentation remains, it may not be fresh enough.[42] To play it safe, buy your meat from a trusted butcher who slices meat uniformly and who cares about providing quality items to customers.

Your butcher will be able to suggest cuts that are not too expensive but still tender enough to enjoy grilled or in a stew or soup. Cheaper cuts are not as tender as expensive ones from the loin, rib, or rump, but you can make the best of them by using a slow cooker.

What Are "Best Before" and "Use by" Dates?

The reason why planning your meals in advance is so important is it helps you avoid buying too much food only to end up throwing it away. The "best before" date gives you information about the quality of food. You can eat food past this date if it looks, smells, and tastes good. The "use-by" date gives you key

---

42 TNN, 2017.

information on safety. You should not eat food past this date because it could be unsafe.

The use by (or expiration) date is clearly stamped on the package. Sometimes, there are symbols (one typical symbol is that of an open can and a symbol like 1M, 2M, or 3M). This means that you should consume the item within one month, two months, or three months (respectively), after opening.

Fun Fact: In the US, food waste is estimated at between 30% to 40% of the food supply, and this means food that could have helped families in need winds up in landfills. Consumers are partially to blame. Problems can also occur at the farming, transporting, and retail stages.[43]

How to Clean and Store Produce

In general, you should wash produce just before you eat it so it does not wilt. Some fruits (like apples and avocados) go brown if you cut them a long time before you eat them, so don't peel or slice them until the moment you are ready to eat them.

All produce, but especially leafy vegetables such as lettuce, spinach, and kale, should be washed thoroughly, as they may contain dirt. Simply place the vegetables under plain running water. There is no need to use soap or produce wash. Use a soft vegetable brush to scrub hard produce like cucumbers and melons. Dry fruits and vegetables afterward with a clean towel or paper towels.[44]

---

43 U.S. Department of Agriculture, n.d.
44 U.S. Food & Drug Administration, n.d.

> **Handy Tip for Root Vegetables Like Carrots:**
> Chop their ends off before washing and peeling them.

Place most vegetables (like root vegetables, cabbage, and celery) in a plastic bag or container in your fridge's crisper drawer. Store vegetables in a different drawer than fruit. Mushrooms are freshest when they are kept in a paper bag.

Store eggs in the fridge, too. If you are iffy about whether they are expired, do the float test. Expired eggs will float to the top or tilt upward, while fresh ones will sink to the bottom of a glass filled with water.

Freezer Storage

Many vegetables can be frozen if you cannot eat them in time. Blanch them before you freeze them to retain their quality. Blanching just means boiling them for one to two minutes and then placing them in ice-cold water to stop the cooking process. You can then dry them and place them in an airtight bag or container in the freezer for up to one year.

> **Handy Tip:** Some vegetables do not maintain a good texture when frozen. These include eggplant, lettuce, potatoes (except mashed potatoes), radishes, sweet potatoes, and artichokes.[45]

---

[45] Unlock Food, n.d.

If you have purchased a meat item that will expire in a few days and you don't think you will be cooking it before then, freeze it as soon as possible. This can extend its shelf life considerably. Fresh meat can last for four to twelve months in a 0°F freezer, while hamburgers or other ground meats last for three to four months. FoodSafety.gov has a thorough "Cold Food Storage Chart" that tells you how long different foods should be kept in the fridge. For instance, hot dogs in an unopened package can last for around two weeks, but once they are open, they last only one week.

Throwing a Dinner Party: Four Easy-to-Prepare Dishes

It is time to knock the socks off your friends and/or family by throwing them a dinner party. Below are four dishes you can use to start your collection of recipes. All recipes serve four diners.

Starter: Avocado With a Vinaigrette Dressing

Ingredients:

- 2 ripe avocados
- ½ cup extra-virgin olive oil
- 1 teaspoon mustard
- 2 tablespoons freshly squeezed lemon juice
- salt and pepper to taste

Instructions:

Make the vinaigrette first, opening the avocados at the last minute because avocados oxidize (go brown) very quickly.

1. Mix all the ingredients except the avocado and adjust to your taste.
2. Slice the avocados in half lengthwise.
3. Insert a sharp knife into the seed and remove it.
4. Pour the vinaigrette into the gaps left by the seed.

Serve with freshly baked bread rolls or toasted bread with the crust removed.

Main Dish: Sautéed Chicken With Peppers

Ingredients for the Marinade:

- 4 chicken breasts cut into one-inch pieces
- 3 tablespoons low-salt soy sauce
- 2 teaspoons minced garlic
- 1 tablespoon toasted sesame oil

Ingredients for the Sauté:

- ½ cup plum sauce
- 3 tablespoons low-salt soy sauce
- ⅓ cup water
- 2 tablespoons lemon juice
- 2 teaspoons ground pepper
- 3 tablespoons avocado or olive oil
- 3 tablespoons cornstarch
- 2 small bell peppers (red and yellow or red and green)
- 1 large onion chopped into small pieces
- 2 large garlic cloves finely chopped

Instructions:

Marinate the chicken for about half an hour in the soy sauce, garlic, and olive oil (you can also do this overnight to save time the next day).

1. Mix the plum sauce, soy sauce, water, lemon juice and pepper with one tablespoon of the cornstarch.

2. Add the two remaining tablespoons of cornstarch to the marinated chicken, ensuring all pieces are evenly coated.
3. Heat two tablespoons of oil in a stir-fry pan and cook the chicken for around four minutes on each side.
4. Set the chicken aside, add the remaining oil, and stir-fry the peppers and onions for about two minutes.
5. Add the garlic and cook for about a minute.
6. Add the chicken pieces you have set aside back into the pan. The sauce will take around two minutes to thicken.

When it's done, it's ready to serve. This dish is best served with a salad or steamed/boiled white rice.

Side Dish: Tomato and Mozzarella Salad With Balsamic Glaze

Ingredients:

- 2 large tomatoes
- 2 large, fresh mozzarella balls (these are white, soft, and packaged in a watery liquid to keep them fresh and soft)
- 1 big bunch of fresh basil leaves
- balsamic glaze to taste
- extra-virgin olive oil to taste
- salt and freshly cracked pepper to taste

Instructions:

1. Slice the tomatoes and mozzarella into thin rounds (around ¼-inch thick).
2. Arrange in a tray placing one slice tomato, one slice mozzarella, then basil leaves, and proceeding in this order until the tray is full.
3. Next, drizzle your creation with olive oil and your balsamic glaze.
4. Season with salt and pepper.

Handy Tip: You can make your own balsamic glaze by heating balsamic vinegar in a saucepan over medium-low heat for around half an hour or until it becomes thick and glaze-like. Keep an eye on it as it could burn if let over the fire too long.

Dessert: Raw Apple Pie

Ingredients for the Crust:

- 2 ¼ cups almonds (crushed or placed in a food processor until they are crumbly)
- 2 cups pitted Medjool dates (These are super-plump and soft, and they blend with other ingredients more smoothly than other dates).

Ingredients for the Filling:

- 4 apples finely sliced
- 1 tablespoon ground cinnamon
- 1 pinch nutmeg

Ingredients for the Syrup:

- ¾ cup pitted dates
- ¾ cup freshly squeezed orange juice
- a little water if needed to thin the syrup

Instructions:

1. For the crust, blend the almonds and dates and pack them on the bottom of a standard-sized pie pan.
2. For the syrup, blend the dates, orange juice, and water (if required) in a blender or using a hand blender.
3. For the pie filling, toss the apples with the cinnamon and nutmeg. Place in fine layers on

top of the crust, alternating layers with syrup so the apple slices stick together.
Place in the refrigerator and serve.

Make Your Dinner Party Special

Add ambience to your party by decorating your table with pretty table runners, decorative pieces, candles, and flowers. Play music everyone loves, ensuring the volume is not too high. Bring out your best dishes and cutlery, to up the elegance factor. Make everyone cookies they can take home as favors.

1. You can store meat in the freezer for up to _____ months.
2. You should wash produce with _____.
3. Organic vegetables have more _____ than conventionally grown produce.
4. Vegetables like (name three) _____ should not be frozen.
5. "Best before" means_____ while "use by" means_____.

   Best Before: _____

   Use by: _____

Human beings cannot survive with great food alone. They also need to live in a clean environment. In the next chapter, I will give you handy tips on how to keep your home clean and tidy.

Before inviting your friends over, make sure your home is clean, tidy, and fragrant. In the next chapter, I will teach you the basics of keeping your home in tip-top condition.

Test Answers:

1. four to twelve months
2. water
3. antioxidants
4. lettuce, kale, and eggplants
5. The quality of the product is best before a specific date, but you can still eat it after if it looks, smells, and tastes okay. "Use by" means food is not safe after the date indicated on the package.

Chapter Five: Keeping Your Home Clean and Tidy

"Cleanliness is a mindset—a positive habit that keeps the body, mind, and environment happy, healthy, simple, neat, and delightful."

–Amit Ray

L iving away from home can feel amazing in the beginning. Finally, you are the master of your universe, and mom and dad are no longer nagging you to pick your shirts up from the floor or wash the dirty dishes in the sink. Trust me, the euphoria will be short-lived if you don't stick to a regular cleaning schedule. Living in a space with dishes piled high or dirt on the floor and other surfaces can get really depressing. Not only that; it can also cause you to fall prey to stomach bugs, allergies, and other health issues that make life a little less rosy.

In case you still need convincing, take a look at the following facts:
- The average faucet has around 6,267 bacteria per square inch, while a typical bath has around 120,000 bacteria per square inch.[46]
- Germs are not only abundant, but they are also long-lasting. For instance, germs like E. coli and salmonella (which both cause major tummy upset) can survive for as long as four hours.[47]

---

[46] Downey, 2017.
[47] Bathroom City, n.d.

To keep diseases at bay when you move into a new apartment, establish a regular cleaning routine and be smart about cleaning.

Invest in Good Equipment

You can buy a vacuum cleaner for as little as $100; though, if you can buy a more powerful one, by all means do. The EPA warns that the air quality in American homes can be up to five times worse than the air quality outdoors.[48] Some of the biggest contributors to indoor air pollution include cleaning products like bleach, grease cleaners, and ammonia. With a good steam vacuum, you won't need much more than water and your machine. Very cheap machines don't have much power, so to really suck up all the dirt and particles that could cause disease, a machine needs to have a good motor. Consider buying a semi-new, second-hand vacuum and/or visit as many garage sales as you can in case a neighbor has a quality piece of equipment you can use.

Buy Green Products or Make Your Own DIY Cleaning Products

When you're at the supermarket, don't make the mistake of popping the first cleaning products you see labeled "bathroom cleaner" or "oven cleaner" into your cart. Educate yourself on eco-friendly household cleaning supplies that are effective yet non-toxic. Some green cleaning products can be considerably more expensive than conventional ones, but if you have respiratory issues like asthma, sensitive skin, or allergies, you may find that the investment is more than worth it.

Also, not all green cleaning brands cost a fortune. Research what is available at nearby stores and supermarkets and

---

[48] United States Environmental Protection Agency, n.d.

conduct searches online to see if bulk buys may be more cost-effective. Just a few of the many green brands known for their affordability include Grove Co., Aunt Fannie's, Seventh Generation, Bon Ami, and Ecos.

DIY Cleaning Products

You can also find big savings by making your own eco-friendly cleaning products. Below you will find three useful, DIY cleaning blends, but there are so many cool "recipes" online for nearly every kind of home cleaning need.

DIY Surface and Window Cleaner
Ingredients:
- 1 cup distilled white vinegar
- 4 cups water
- 15 drops of your favorite essential oil

Instructions:
1. Pour all the ingredients into a spray bottle.
2. Start cleaning!

DIY Oven Cleaner
Ingredients:
- ¼ cup baking soda
- water

Instructions:
1. Mix enough water into the baking soda to make a thick paste.
2. Cover the area of grease for a few hours or overnight.
3. Wipe off with a wet cloth or paper towel.

DIY Bathroom Cleaner

Ingredients:
- 2 cups baking soda
- ¾ cup warm water
- ¾ cup liquid dishwashing liquid
- 3 tablespoons white distilled vinegar

Instructions:
1. Mix the ingredients in a jar.
2. Remove any signs of mildew or dirt on grout.

Use Natural Instead of Synthetic Fragrances and Burn Natural Candles

Whether you have friends coming over or you simply enjoy studying or working in a fragrant home, rely on the power of essential oils. With the help of a small electric essential oil diffuser, you can fill an entire room with beautiful fragrances that have no toxic ingredients. Choose therapeutic-grade oils like lavender and orange to calm you and boost your mood. If you love scented candles, go for beeswax or soy candles; these do not contain formaldehyde or other potential toxins (unlike some paraffin candles).

Establish a Cleaning Routine

Cleaning the same spaces on the same day, at the same time will ensure you don't let hygiene slide, and it will make cleaning less stressful. A typical cleaning schedule might look something like this:[49]

---

[49] McDonough & Picard, 2019.

Cleaning Routine

Everyday:

- Make your bed.
- Wipe down the kitchen countertop and cupboards.
- Do the dishes.
- Sweep the kitchen floors.
- Sanitize the kitchen and bathroom floors.

Once a month:

- Dust you blinds.
- Clean your dishwasher, laundy machine and vacuum.
- Dust your lamps and lighting fixtures.

Every three months:

- Wash soft furnishing like comforters and pillows.
- Descale your coffee maker.
- Clean your oven.
- Reorganize your freezer.
- Clean the interior of your car with a hand vacuum cleaner.
- Wipe the inside of the fridge. Remove trays from the fridge and give them a good wash with hot water and soap.
- Vacuum your mattress.

Every year:

- Have a deep clean of areas like the kitchen chimney,drapes, curtains and gutter.
- Have a spring cleaning session,clearing out, wardrobes, the kitchen storage cabinets and every nook and crannies of the house.

How to Do the Laundry

The way you do your laundry will vary depending on the machine you have, but the good news is that most machines have symbols that are easy to understand. They represent different cycles (both short and long) which you can select, depending on how dirty your clothes are or how delicate/sturdy their fabrics are.

Checking Symbols on Clothing

Before washing any items of clothing, you should read the symbols that appear on the tags. Typical symbols include:

- The degrees at which clothing should be washed.

- Instructions regarding the need to wash the item on a gentle/wool wash cycle.
- The need to hand-wash items.
- The need to dry-clean items.
- Instructions not to wring items when wet (as they could become deformed).

Research any symbol you do not understand. Some are a bit tricky. For instance, a red triangle with an X across it means you should NOT bleach. A green triangle means bleaching is allowed, and a green triangle with diagonal green stripes means you should use a non-chlorine bleach.

Clothing also comes with drying labels. When you see a green square with three vertical stripes, it means the items should be air-dried. All these symbols are explained on many sites— including those belonging to companies that make clothes washing products.[50]

Also, pay attention to the ironing instructions. Be careful of a red iron symbol that is crossed out by an X. It means you should NOT iron the outfit. There is another important symbol: that of a red iron with two vertical lines beneath it, which are crossed out by an X. It means you should not steam the product.

Finally, check if your outfit should be dry-cleaned. If you see a green circle with no frame, it means the item should be dry-cleaned. A red circle with an X across it, meanwhile, means you should not dry-clean the item. If you see a red circle within a square frame and an X across it, you should not tumble-dry it.

---

[50] Ariel, n.d.

Using the Washing Machine

The instructions for using a washing machine will vary slightly depending on the model you have. The following tips will help ensure your clothes are kept in good condition and do not fade or stain:

- Separate colored items from whites.
- Turn clothes right side out.
- Read labels and follow instructions regarding temperature, handwashing, and similar.
- Pre-treat stains with a good stain remover.
- Put the clothing in the washer, ensuring you do not overfill. Add detergent and fabric softener.
- Hang clothes out to dry or place them in the dryer, checking the lint filter and clearing it. Use the right level of heat so clothes are not damaged.
- Fold clothing and place the same type of item in the same spot in your wardrobe.

How to Iron Clothes

To look smart, your clothing should be wrinkle-free. The following tips will ensure you look as stylish on the outside as you feel on the inside:[51]

- Irons get piping hot in a matter of seconds, so make sure never to put your idle hand down on the ironing board.
- Set the temperature of the iron according to the fabric you are ironing.
- Use the spray setting on your iron to eliminate wrinkles faster.

---

[51] Teen Toolkit, 2017.

- Turn clothes inside-out to iron them if they have prints or stickers on them.
- Do not iron anything while you are wearing it.

How to Remove Stains

Each stain type is a world unto its own; what works for one type of stain won't necessarily work for another. Below you will find a few instructions for tackling typically tough stains. When in doubt, ask and search. Don't risk destroying clothing by scrubbing with abrasive brushes, steel wool, or other items you may use to clean the rest of your home.

Grass: This is easily one of the toughest stains to remove, because the chlorophyll in grass discolors clothing very quickly. Spray the stain with a pre-wash solution, pop it into the machine using an enzyme detergent (which helps break down soils and stains), and wash it on the hottest possible temperature the fabric can endure.

Felt-Tip Marker: Mix two tablespoons of liquid dishwashing detergent and two tablespoons of white vinegar with two-and-a-half cups of warm water. Using a clean white cloth, apply the solution to the stain. Blot it repeatedly with a dry cloth until the stain disappears. Flush with clear water.

Grease: For fresh stains, sprinkle baking soda on top of the grease. For older stains, pour dishwashing soap on the stain and leave it for around 10 minutes. Scrub it off with a toothbrush. You may need to repeat this several times so the baking soda can soak up all the grease.

Lipstick: Take a cotton ball or swab and dampen it with rubbing alcohol. Blot the stain with the alcohol and rub until the lipstick comes off. Rinse the item out with cool water and machine-wash it.

Glue: Nail polish remover with acetone usually works great with this type of stain. Dip a cotton ball or swab in acetone and gently rub the stain. Drop some laundry detergent into the stain, rub it in with another cotton ball, and leave it for a bit. Machine-wash the items as usual, and the stain should be completely gone.

How to Restore Brightness to Whites

Pristine white clothing can lose its pure hue after washing, especially if you have ever washed it with colored clothing. To restore whites to their original beauty, try a DIY solution comprised of one cup of baking soda and one gallon of warm water. Leave the clothing to soak for eight hours or more and machine-wash as usual. You can also buy handy whitening products with labels like "laundry whitener and stain remover" written on their labels. These typically come in pod or powder form.

Next, fill your washing machine with warm water, selecting the soak cycle. Let the clothing soak for about six hours or longer. If you don't have a soak setting on your washing machine, just use a bucket or even your bathtub to soak clothes for hours. Just make sure they are totally submerged. Next, machine-wash your whites with a little bleach powder for clothing. Don't use too much; follow the instructions. Some bleach powders indicate you should add the powder a few minutes after the cycle has started. If the clothes tag permits it, wash the item in hot water and choose a "soil" cycle (which is used for clothes that are very dirty). Wash as usual and you will notice that your shirts and socks are sparkling white!

A True Story: Claire always gets mad at me when I tell this story, but I just can't help it. It's too much fun to keep all to ourselves. I remember that when Claire met her boyfriend, she was super excited to go on her first date with him. He was taking her to the ballet and a fancy dinner, and she had the perfect dress for the occasion—a designer dress she had worn to her cousin's wedding. It was made of silk and was simple but chic.

Claire had thought that the dress was in perfect condition, but the morning of her date, she discovered an unsightly spot in the middle of it. *No worries*, she thought, she would wash it and pop it in the dryer, and it would be ready in no time. Her dress came out clean as a whistle, of course, but there was just one problem: it had shrunk to Barbie doll size (I exaggerate, but you get my drift). This was another "panic moment" that she survived thanks to the help of her roommate, who lent her a dress. These days, Claire is super careful to read the labels, which just goes to show that your biggest disasters are often the best ways to pick up good habits.

Test time!

It is once again time to show you remember the most important points of this chapter. Check your answers at the end of the chapter.

1. How often should you wipe your kitchen countertops and cupboards?
    a. Once a week
    b. Every day
    c. Once a month
2. How often should you dust your furniture?
    a. Every two days
    b. Every day

c. Once a week
3. How often should you mop the floors?
    a. Every day
    b. Every two days
    c. Once a week
4. What does a red circle within a frame and an X across it on a clothing tag mean?
    a. It should not be ironed.
    b. It should not be steam-cleaned.
    c. It should not be tumble-dried.
5. What does a green square with three vertical stripes mean?
    a. The item of clothing should be air-dried.
    b. It should be dry-cleaned.
    c. It should be washed on a gentle cycle.

Now that your house is looking spick and span, it is time to work on your personal style routine! This may seem like a chore at first, but you will soon find that it's one of the most rewarding parts of your day!

Test Answers:
    1. b
    2. a
    3. c
    4. c
    5. a

Chapter Six: Building a Fashionable, Practical Wardrobe

"Style is a way to say who you are without having to speak."

–Rachel Zoe

Whether you're a freshman at college or you're starting a new job, it's important to look fashionable and well-put-together. In fact, expert stylists often say that you should dress like the person you want to be. Looking smart can give you the confidence you need to reach for your goals. In this chapter, you will learn how to build a wardrobe of basics for all major occasions.

Seven Seconds Away

Did you know that you have just seven seconds to make a great impression on others?[52] In this short amount of time, people can make a judgment about what you are like, and it can be very difficult to prove them wrong later. First impressions are long-lasting, and you don't want to miss out on a  promotion or a date with someone you are interested in because you are looking less like your best. You don't need to spend a lot of money or rack up a big carbon footprint to be fashionable.

---

[52] Gibbons, 2018.

In fact, you can do so sustainably and responsibly with just a few dollars!

Wardrobe Essentials

Whether you are still at home, getting ready to leave for college, or starting a job, the list of "must-have" items for your wardrobe include:[53]

- jeans
- workout gear
- simple everyday tops, both with and without a collar
- sweatshirts
- sweaters
- a few casual yet stylish dresses or trousers paired with tops
- at least one dark or neutral pant/skirt suit (Eventually, aim to have about five skirts and/or pairs of pants plus a few blouses and/or shirts you can mix and match.)
- a couple of good white blouses/dress shirts
- a couple of professional-looking but fashionable blazers
- a good pair of dress shoes
- pajamas
- a couple of winter coats (one dressier, one casual)
- boots and socks (summer and winter)
- thermal underwear (if necessary)
- at least one cocktail dress and one long dress for formal or gala events

---

[53] Fashion Week Online, n.d.

Prioritizing Quality

It's perfectly fine to occasionally buy trendy items, but most of the clothing in your wardrobe should be made of quality fabrics that are comfortable and resilient. For instance, if you are working out, choosing items that wick away sweat can make a big difference to your performance and even your motivation to make an extra effort during your routine or during sporting competitions.

Signs That Items Are Durable and Built to Last

You don't need to buy brand items or take a manufacturer's word for it to know if clothing is good-quality or not. The following details indicate the item you are eyeing is worth the expense:

- The stitching is even and straight.
- You cannot see through the fabric.
- When you pull at the seams, no gaps appear.
- The fabric pattern meets evenly at the seams.
- Hems are well-finished.
- The fabric doesn't wrinkle easily.
- Collared shirts have an extra panel of material that strengthens them.
- Zippers are hidden and well-stitched.
- The material retains its shape after being tugged.
- Extra buttons and thread are provided.
- The product comes with a warranty.

High-quality clothing is usually a little more expensive, but it will stand the test of time so you don't have to shop so frequently.

Timing Your Purchases

You can score big savings by making a list of desired items and buying them during summer sales and Black Friday and post-Christmas sales. Stick to your list so you don't overspend during sales periods. Typically, big-name retailers offer the best deals. Amazon is another big favorite because it offers discounts on a wide range of items.

If you are sales shopping online, make sure you aren't taken for a ride. Some sites announce big discounts but actually list items at the same price you can find them everywhere else without a discount. Never buy an item from the first site you see. Do a quick search to see the price at which other retailers are selling your chosen item.

Fun Fact: Why is the special once-a-year sale called Black Friday? The term "Black Friday" first appeared in the journal *Factory Management and Maintenance*. It was used to describe the day after Thanksgiving, when many employees would call in sick so they could have an extra free day off[54]. US police officers also used this term to describe the big traffic jams that would start as soon as the Christmas shopping season commenced. Many stores were excited by the idea of starting sales as early as after Thanksgiving, offering shoppers prices that were too tempting to resist.

[54] Lee, 2017.

Embracing Sustainable Fashion

The fashion industry is responsible for up to 10% of global carbon emissions and 20% of wastewater. What makes fashion so problematic is that it encourages a frenetic pace, pushing consumers to buy new items every season if they want to stay on trend. There are so many ways that the clothing industry contributes to global warming. For instance, to make just one pair of jeans, around 2.2 pounds of cotton are required.[55] Because cotton tends to grow in dry environments, this amount of cotton alone requires up to 2,642 gallons of water. This is equivalent to what one person drinks in ten years.

Emissions are another big problem. Around one-third of emissions are produced by fiber and fabric production, 8% can be attributed to the manufacture of the jeans in the above example; 16% is caused by packaging, transport, and retails; and 40% comes from the consumer (who washes the jeans and eventually dumps them in a landfill).

Many surveys show that people wear t-shirts about 22 times a year but wear dresses only ten times a year. The more you wear an item, the lower its CO2 footprint becomes because you don't have to buy new items to replace it. Surveys also show that one-fifth of items owned by US consumers are never worn.

What Can You Do to Help?

In order to reduce your CO2 footprint, aim to:

- Visit shops and try clothing on. Buying clothes online can theoretically save you from travelling to shops, but the truth is that many people return items of clothing if

---

[55] Ro, 2020.

they do not fit properly. Therefore, travel emissions are doubled or sometimes tripled.

- Try to buy quality items you won't need to replace every year.
- Opt for classic styles, using accessories and smaller items to be more in line with seasonal trends.
- Recycle items. Organize clothes swap days with your friends, consider shopping at vintage shops, and upcycle old items. Learning to sew can be a big help when it comes to jazzing up or mending items.
- Back sustainable clothing brands. There is a myriad of brands that are creating beautiful, eco-friendly fashions. The list includes Patagonia, Stella McCartney, and Bureo. The latter works alongside fishing communities in South America, collecting, cleaning, and shredding fishing nets to recycle them into NetPlus® – a material whose production provides supplemental income to local communities while also providing raw material to other brands.

Patagonia is a particularly proactive brand. It is piloting its first cotton crop in India on over 150 farms. In doing this, they are rehabilitating soil, respecting animal welfare, and helping boost the local economies.

Companies like Eileen Fisher, meanwhile, are embracing the "circular by design" concept, collecting discarded items from their own brand and re-manufacturing them into brand-new designs.[56]

Some companies (including Roya Aghighi) are making "living clothing." This brand has developed a living, biodegradable fabric called "biogarmentry" that is made

---

[56] Gerholdt, 2017.

from algae. The fabric takes in carbon and emits oxygen, thus helping to purify air. Also called a "photosynthesizing textile," biogarmentry can't be washed. To keep it in good shape, all you need to do is spray it with water.

Dressing for the Occasion

Make sure you dress appropriately for every occasion. If you are invited to an elegant dinner, for instance, feel free to ask the host about the dress code. You may be expected to wear a suit and tie, in which case the formal outfit that is hanging in your wardrobe will be perfect. When in doubt, ask friends, teachers, and people in your circle for advice. If you are going on an excursion, ask for the itinerary beforehand so you dress right for the occasion.

This doesn't mean you have to forego your personality. Fashion is a means of personal expression, so make sure your outfit says something about your aspirations, goals, and personality.

A True Story: It's time to take the heat off Claire now and talk about myself. I'll never forget the time I was invited to a party at a beach club when I was on vacation with my husband. Our friends told us it was a "gold party," and I thought that meant you had to wear a gold accessory. I wore a gold cuff that I bought at a vintage shop earlier that day. Imagine my surprise when I was rejected at the door. Guests were required to dress in gold clothing, not just wear golden accessories. I ended up having a great time anyway. We dined by the sea and watched the fireworks being lit from the very beach club that had rejected us. My friends told me there was great live music and that a few celebrities showed up at the event we missed. Sometimes, dress codes can be very strict, so it can be worth your while to call the venue beforehand to find out what is expected.

1. Which of these items is not considered a "must-have" for your college wardrobe?
   a. Jeans
   b. Sweatshirts
   c. A jumpsuit
2. What is one sign that an item of clothing is good quality?
   a. It is expensive.
   b. The fabric pattern matches up at the seams.
   c. The fabric is thin.
3. What percentage of global carbon emissions does the fashion industry cause?
   a. 10%
   b. 50%
   c. 80%
4. Which of these brands makes living clothing?
   a. Roya Aghigi
   b. Eileen Fisher
   c. Stella McCartney
5. What does "circular by design" mean in the fashion world?
   a. Clothing items can be returned to a designer for remanufacturing and recycling.
   b. Clothing with the green circle symbol on the tag
   c. Wearing photosynthesizing items

Now that you look the part, you should ensure that your car is up to par. In the next chapter, you will learn to perform basic car maintenance duties. This way, you will feel safe and secure every time you hit the road.

Test Answers:
1. c
2. b
3. a
4. a
5. a

Chapter Seven: Car Maintenance Tips

"Everything in life is somewhere else, and you get there in a car."

–E. B. White

One of the most liberating things about being an older teen is driving your first car. Your first set of wheels will enable you to go more places, visit friends who may live a little distance away, and access places that don't have great public transportation. Make sure you keep your vehicle in good working order by following important maintenance tips.

Fun Facts:

- Around 52% of teens aged 15 to 17 don't know how to replace a tire. Some 32% don't know how to check tire pressure, and 44% don't know how to inspect the state of their tire tread—as found in a survey by Michelin and the Fédération Internationale de l'Automobile.[57]
- Around 81% of Americans have had a flat tire.[58]
- There are 69 million vehicle breakdowns in the US every year (which is equivalent to one in three drivers).[59]
- 150 million people sit in traffic caused by breakdowns every year.
- Many injuries and even fatalities are caused every year while people are trying to resolve a breakdown.

---

[57] Bennett, 2014.
[58] After Market News, 2019.
[59] Agero Insights, 2019.

You should take your car for a professional check-up and maintenance as often as your car manufacturer prescribes. They may suggest that you take your car in every year or after you have driven a specific number of miles. The older your car is, the more frequently a check-up will be required. You can actually take care of a few maintenance issues yourself as well. Some of the most important ones are listed below.

Skills Every Teen Should Know

I'm going to be honest with you—I'm not the biggest metal head, and I'm no Louis Hamilton on the road. I got my license when I was relatively "old" (I was 26), and I only did so because I started working half an hour from where I lived, and public transport availability was poor. Everything about cars scared me when I was younger (the sheer weight of the car, the amount of grease involved in maintenance, and the challenge of using a gauge and knowing when to stop)! One thing that really surprised me, though, is how addictive car maintenance can become. Once you master tasks like changing a tire, filling a tire with air, or changing your wiper fluid, you get quite excited about performing maintenance work.

Claire and Neil are my opposites, as they love working beneath a car, getting their hands dirty, and knowing about the inner workings of a motor. I may not be at their level, but I am happy to say I now do all my own small maintenance work. I still leave the big stuff (like replacing brake disks, checking the battery, and ensuring filters are still working) to my mechanic.

I have compiled a list of essential skills you need from the very first day you get behind a wheel. Never allow yourself to be insecure, scared, or in a panic. Stay on top of things; don't let them wrest from your peace of mind or sense of safety.

Checking Liquid Levels

Your oil and coolant levels should be well topped-up. Check oil levels every four to six weeks and coolant levels every couple of weeks. As for your wiper fluid, the frequency of check-ups depends on how often you use it. Generally, you should check it every two months or so. You will notice when liquid levels are low, as the liquid will come with less pressure.

Checking Oil Levels

To check the oil, first, warm up the car and then turn it off. Open the hood and use the hood prop to keep it open so you can get to work. Look for the oil dipstick. It usually has a yellow or orange circular handle that is easy to find. When you pull it, a long metal stick will slide out of the engine. Clean the dipstick and reinsert it into the engine. Ensure that the oil reaches the required level on the dipstick. If the level is low but the oil is clean, add new oil. If the oil is gritty, it needs to be changed. I personally don't believe in changing oil yourself, because sometimes, the filter is also dirty and needs to be changed. I suggest that if the oil is gritty, you take your car to the mechanic for an oil and filter change.

Checking Coolant Levels

WARNING: Never check your coolant levels when your car's engine is hot. Pressure can build up in the reservoir, and the hot liquid can spurt out and cause burns.

Car engine coolant, also called antifreeze, protects engines from overheating. It also prevents damage to the water pump, head gasket, piston timing, and cylinder, and it lubricates the moving components that come into contact with your engine.

To check the coolant level, open the hood and prop it up. Look for the coolant reservoir. It is typically easy to find because it will say "coolant" on the cap. If you cannot find it, read the car manual, which will indicate where the coolant reservoir is. When you find the reservoir, you will see that it has "full" and "low" levels embossed on its side. The reservoir is translucent, and the fluid is usually greenish so you can clearly see when a top-up is required. If the coolant level is closer to the "low" mark, it is time to add some coolant to the reservoir.

Open the cap with a rag, take the coolant recommended for your car, and use a funnel to pour the liquid in. Add enough coolant until you reach the "full" mark.

Changing the Windshield Wiper Fluid

You will need to buy a specific fluid to clean your windshield optimally. You can find this fluid just about anywhere, including the grocery store, gas station, or local convenience store.

To refill wiper fluid, check your owner's manual to locate the windshield wiper fluid container. Open the hood and prop it up. It usually features a bright cap with an embossed image of a windshield. Remove the lid and place it in a safe spot. Using a funnel, fill the container until it reaches the "full" or "filled" line. If there is no visible line, just leave about two inches of free space. Replace the cap and lower the hood.

Caring for Tires

Your car's display will usually inform you when you need to fill your tires with air. A symbol or text reminder will pop up on your dashboard indicating the pressure on one or more tires is low.

When this happens, cool your tires down before making your way to the nearest gas station and using the dedicated air pump.

The first step is to find out what pressure your tires should have. This information is located on a sticker on the interior side of the driver's door. The sticker will inform you of how much pressure your front, back, and spare tires should have. For instance, your sticker may indicate that your front tires should have a 35 PSI and your back tires should also have a 35 PSI.

Useful definition: PSI refers to the minimum amount of air pressure needed to support your vehicle at its maximum load. You should park your car close enough to the air pump machine so that the gauge can reach all tires.

Useful Fact: Not all gasoline stations have air available. Some provide free air, while others require you to pay a coin or two into the machine before it provides air.

Before placing your dollar into the air pressure machine, unscrew the air valve steam caps on all your tires. Most air pump machines work similarly. You indicate the pressure you want your tires to have and subsequently press the tip of the nozzle firmly against the air valve. The machine will continue to deliver air until your chosen pressure level is reached and then beep to let you know it's time to remove the hose. Cover all the valves once again, and you're ready to go.

Checking Tire Pressure

If you will be taking a road trip, it is a good idea to check your tire pressure first. Tires with low pressure can add to your fuel bill and lead to accidents.[60] You can check the pressure by using a tire gauge, which you can buy at any auto store or online. Prices range from $5 for a basic gauge to around $30 for a digital one. Unscrew the valve stem, press the pressure gauge into the air valve, and remove the gauge to read the pressure.

Checking Your Tire Tread Depth

This is an easy and fun task. To gauge your tire tread depth, simply stick a penny into the groove with Abraham Lincoln's head upside down and facing you. If you can see the president's entire head, your tire tread depth is less than 2/32 inch, and it's time to replace your tire.[61] You should check your tire depth approximately every 3,000 miles or once it reaches 4/32 inches deep. When the tread depth reaches 2/32 inches, it's time for a tire replacement.

Changing a Flat Tire

Even if your tires are in good shape, you never know when you might drive over a nail or another sharp object and need to replace a flat tire. If a tire goes flat, drive your car to a safe place before attempting to change it. Carry road flares in case you need to stop on the road and turn on your four-way hazards as well. Make yourself as visible as possible to avoid accidents.

> **Useful Tip:** If you get a flat, do not panic. Usually, your car can chug ahead for a bit before it is unable to move. Prioritize safety above all things. Find a safe spot if you can—such as the parking lot of a mall or a gasoline station. Many fatal accidents and injuries occur when people try to

---

[60] Parra, 2021.
[61] Good Year, n.d.

> change their tires while on a dangerous or heavily
> travelled part of the road.

The spare tire is typically located under the floorboard in the trunk. Bring it out and set it next to the tire you wish to change. Take a lug wrench and loosen the lug nuts on your tire. Raise the car with a jack only as much as you need to (the tire should be an inch or two off the ground, no more). Remove the flat tire, insert the spare one, and half-tighten the lug nuts (do not tighten all the way yet). Lower the vehicle, keep the jack in your car, and tighten the lug nuts fully.[62]

Checking the Lights

Before you go out at night or on a road trip, make sure all your lights are working. Just turn on your car in a garage or another dark place, since in broad daylight it can sometimes be difficult to see if the lights are on or off. If a headlight is broken, know that it's easy to change. Most bulbs are of the halogen high-intensity discharge (HID) or light-emitting diode (LED) variety. Both these bulb types are kept in place with thin wire clips or rotating retainers. You can pop them out from behind the headlight and replace them with a click. It is a good idea to keep a couple of light replacements in your car. Check the manual so you know which lights to buy.[63]

Checking Your Wiper Blades

It is important for your wiper blades to be in perfect working order because if not, they can cause streaks or fail to eliminate rain adequately, making it harder to see the road when it is rainy. To make sure your wiper blades are working well, inspect them

---

[62] Drive Safely, n.d.
[63] Keebler, 2019.

by lifting them into an upright position. Check to see if the blade is damaged or deformed. The blades are usually replaced by simply sliding them off and sliding the new ones on. However, you need to make sure your replacement blades are the exact same model as your original blades. Most adults take their vehicle to the mechanic for wiper blade replacement, and because they are such an important safety feature, I suggest that you do the same!

A True Story: Claire was driving to her part-time job recently, and she drove over a nail. (Unfortunately, there are many hazards on the road that can cause damage to your tires, including car parts, shards of glass, screws, and other sharp objects.) She was able to pull into the parking lot of a Burger King and change her tire without an issue. I am really pleased that she is so much more capable than I was at her age, but the good news is that even if you start later in life, there is always time to learn and grow!

Jump-Starting a Car

This skill will become a lot less important as more people make the switch to electric cars. However, if you are driving a car with a combustion engine, you should know how to jump-start a car in case your battery dies out. Jump-staring a car can be dangerous, so if this happens to you, contact a roadside assistance professional if possible. However, if you are stranded on a dark road and you want to get out of there, then knowing how to jump-start your vehicle is key.

Step by Step Instructions

To do so, you will need to face your vehicle and the assisting vehicle towards each other and park. Open and prop the hoods and find the batteries. You will see that there are positive and negative battery terminals. Follow these instructions in their precise order:[64]

1. Place the red clamp on the positive post on the dead battery and the other end on the positive post on the working battery.
2. The black jump lead should be placed on the negative terminal of the working battery. The other end should be affixed to a "grounding point" (unpainted metal on the engine or the chassis, far away from the flat battery and the fuel system).
3. Keep both engines off, waiting for around three minutes.
4. Start the engine of the working car and keep it running for around one minute.
5. Turn on the car with the flat battery.
6. Let both cars run for around 10 minutes. Turn off both engines and carefully disconnect the leads in the reverse order from the way you connected them. (Remove the black lead from the assisted car first and finish with the red lead from the assisting car.)
7. Restart your car.

Removing Jump Leads

In case you want the precise order for removing the jump leads, read on:
1. With both engines off, remove the black jump lead from the unpainted metal or grounding point.
2. Remove the other end of the black jump lead from the negative terminal of the assisting battery.
3. Disconnect the red jump lead from the positive terminal of the assisting battery.

---

[64] AA, n.d.

4. Remove the other end of the red jump from the positive terminal on the formerly dead battery.

Starting Your Car With a Battery Booster Pack

If you travel long distances, it is a good idea to keep a battery booster pack in your trunk. This will enable you to jump-start your car even if no vehicle is around that can help you. It is especially helpful for anyone who might be nervous or scared to ask for help from a stranger. The process is similar to what you learned above:

1. Connect the red jump lead from the battery pack to the positive terminal or post of your battery.
2. Connect the black negative jump lead to a grounding point that is far away from the fuel system.
3. Turn on the pack.
4. Try to start the car and keep it running but idle for around five minutes.
5. Turn off the boost pack and warm up the engine for another five or 10 minutes.
6. Turn off the engine and remove the leads in the opposite order to how you placed them (remove the black lead first, then the red one).
7. Restart your car.

Useful Tip: Keep this book in your car so you can pull it out in the case of an emergency. You never know when you might get stuck somewhere with no smartphone coverage.

Test time!

1. How often should you check your oil levels?
   a. Every four to six weeks
   b. Every two weeks
   c. Every day
2. What is the symbol on the cap of the windshield wiper reservoir?
   a. A windshield
   b. A fountain
   c. A symbol of two parallel lines
3. When should you check and change your coolant?
   a. When the engine is hot
   b. When the engine is cold
   c. When the engine has rested for two days
4. What coin should you use to check for tire tread depth?
   a. A penny
   b. A dime
   c. A dollar
5. Should your tires be hot, warm, or cold when you add pressure?
   a. They should be hot.
   b. They should be cold.
   c. They should be warm.

One of the most important experiences many older teens undergo is moving out of their parent's home, either to attend college or simply to experience what it's like to live alone. In the next chapter, I will give you a few tips on how to find a safe and cozy place to live.

Test Answers:
1. a
2. a
3. b
4. a
5. b

Chapter Eight: Moving Out

"If we were meant to stay in one place, we'd have roots instead of feet."

–Rachel Wolchin

Moving out is exciting and stressful all at once. On the one hand, it represents a time of greater independence and individuality. On the other hand, it requires you to be far more responsible for aspects such as paying your rent on time, staying safe, and moving your belongings. Check out the following tips to ensure your move goes without a hitch.

> **Fun Fact:** Research compiled by the US Bureau of Labor Statistics shows[65] that the median age at which young adults move away from their parents' home for a period of at least three months or longer, is 19. If you are around this age, you may have moved out to attend college or work in another city or area. If so, what sort of living arrangement is best for you?

Useful Statistics

If you were wondering what most people your age do when they go off to college, the following statistics may help:

---

[65] U.S. Bureau of Labor Statistics, n.d.

- Only 22% of college students in the US live on-campus. Around 55% live in rented homes, while 23% live in purpose-built, off-campus homes.[66]
- The country's 175 largest universities can provide on-campus accommodations for only 21.5% of undergraduates.
- Around 8.6 million students in the US need rental homes that are located close to their campus.
- For the vast majority of college students, the availability of quality housing is a big decision-maker when it comes to choosing a college.
- The average cost of renting on-campus accommodation amounts to around $7,717 a year.
- Off-campus, student-competitive accommodations have higher yearly rental costs (an average of $13,093 per year).
- Private school housing tends to cost more than public school options.
- Costs of rent can vary greatly depending on the college you attend. For instance, Berkeley, California has off-campus monthly housing costs of around $2,300 per month, while in Tallahassee, Florida, you can pay around $600 for this type of accommodation.

Income Requirements for Rentals

If you want to rent an apartment for the first time, know that landlords can require you to earn three to three-and-a-half times the cost of the rent to consider you for approval. If you have found a nice place, and you do not make as much income as you need to, you can get an adult to co-sign for you and promise to pay the rent if you are unable to.

---

[66] Finances Online, n.d.

Choosing a Safe, Convenient Area

It can be tempting to opt for the cheapest apartment available, but if it is far from your college or your workplace or it is in an unsafe neighborhood, your choice could cost you more money in the long run. You could also risk having your home broken into, and your security could be threatened. Before renting, search online and ask people in the location you will be moving to for a shortlist of recommended, safe, and affordable suburbs.

David Hall, emergency manager at Missouri State University, actually recommends that the smartest move you can make is to visit the local police department. They can advise you on which areas to avoid. They can also provide information on any registered sex offenders living in the area.[67]

Additional Safety Tips

- You should prioritize buildings with a front desk for a security guard or concierge.
- Avoid buildings with exterior hallways, as it can be easier for attackers to surprise dwellers. Interior hallways will keep you safer.
- Avoid buildings that have potentially dangerous or dark areas you have to cross when you're walking home. Trace your route from college and nearby supermarkets to make sure the areas you will tread through are well-lit and populated.
- Try to get an apartment on a higher floor, since first floor or ground-level dwellings are easier to break into.
- Analyze where your apartment is located. Is there a tree or are there high shrubs that would help an intruder break in through a window? Are there numerous trees

---

[67] Coy, 2018.

and shrubs that could serve as hiding spots for criminals?

- Look carefully at the interior of the dwelling, making sure that fixtures and equipment are clean and in good condition. Watch out for mold spores in damp areas like bathrooms and be wary of homes with a musty odor.
- Don't be shy about asking the landlord for inspection reports. All heating devices should be safe, as should electrical and plumbing systems. If you have the budget for it, you can also have a professional maintenance representative accompany you and check out one or two homes you are interested in.
- Ask the landlord if the home has a security system. Ideally, your new apartment should be in a community that has gated access, security professionals, and video cameras. If not, ask if you can pay for a home security system if you have the budget for it. Check that doors are made of quality materials and that they have deadbolts.
- All windows and doors should have secure locks.
- Make sure the entirety of your home is well-lit.
- Install motion detection lights near the entrance to your apartment.
- Build a good relationship with neighbors so you can watch out for each other and report anything that looks suspicious.
- Check all fire escapes and exit doors to ensure they are easily accessible and not locked.
- Take a self-defense class so you feel more confident when you are alone.
- If you are renting a home instead of an apartment, considering installing a smart doorbell. This piece of technology has cameras that enable you to see who is at the door.

Sharing an Apartment

If renting an apartment by yourself is too expensive, you may prefer to share housing with other students or young adults. All tenants' names will need to be on the lease, so ensure that you trust the people you are moving in with. You might also find it convenient to rent a room in an apartment that someone else is renting. In this case, they will be subleasing or subletting the room, but your name will not be on the lease, and you will not be responsible if something goes wrong. Sharing a home has many pros and cons, which you should carefully weigh.[68]

Pros Include:

- You will have people to hang out with.
- You may feel safer because you are not alone.
- You will pay lower costs for renting a home.

Cons Include:

- Living with inconsiderate roommates is an unfortunate possibility.
- You risk living with people whose lifestyle is incompatible with yours.
- Not having privacy when you want it is a likely reality.

Tips for Choosing Roommates

There is no 100% foolproof method for choosing a roommate. In my own experience, there have been times that I have shared a flat with someone I thought would be perfect, only to find that we had totally different expectations regarding so many aspects—including tidiness, visitors, and meal preparation.

---

[68] My Home by Freddie Mac, 2022.

Once, I was desperate to find a flat, and I found an ad on my college noticeboard. It was for a room in an apartment shared by two other girls. I met them, instantly got along with them, moved in, and that year was one of the best of my life. We got on famously and shared expenses for food and even entertainment. We liked each other so much that we even went backpacking and camping together, and I became close to their families as well. I made true friendships that I still hold dear to my heart.

There may be no "one size fits all" solution for finding room/housemates, but the following strategies can be helpful:

- **Talk about cleaning routines.** You will quickly discover if someone does not follow a regular cleaning routine or if they don't value cleanliness, sanitation, and tidiness.
- **Compare your schedules.** If one of your roommates works a night shift and you are away all day, you could still be perfectly compatible. What won't work so well is someone who often throws parties at home and stays up late when you are trying to get quality sleep for a big exam the next day. Compatibility isn't just about lifestyles; it is also about empathy and consideration for your roommates.
- **Rely on help from your college.** Many colleges have systems that connect students with shared interests (including academic subjects and sports). This can be a good bet if you prefer not to live in a rental home with non-students.

Roomate checklist

Finding a roomate:

- Deside what person you would like to have as a roomate.
- Use your network to find suitable people.
- Make sure your potential roommate is legit.
- Get a sense of a potential roommate's finances.
- Invite potential roommates for an interview.

Setting expectations:

- Communicate openly and honestly.
- Decide how you handle rent and utility payments.
- Agree on how you will handle cleaning responsibilities.
- Decide on how you will handle messages and mail.
- Decide who is responsible for calling the landlord in case of any problems.
- Decide if you have to give notice if you will be having visitors.
- Decide if the guests can stay overnight.
- Decide which rooms are considered "common areas".
- Set guidelines regarding private spaces.
- Decide who will be given a key to your apartment.
- Decide if you're willing to share clothing, music, dishes and other items.
- Decide if household supplies will be shared.

A True Story: Claire's best friend, Ellie, was once attacked as she was coming home. It was around 11pm, and her friends had dropped her off at her place. The car pulled out, and as Ellie was walking to the door, someone came up to her quickly, knocking her down with a blow and took her backpack. The bag had her phone and a camera her mom had given her for her birthday. It also had all her semester's notes for a couple of subjects.

Ellie moved out of this place and moved in with another student from her college. The place was well-lit and had security. Ellie went the extra mile, though, learning self-defense. She told me that in her course, she learned to look out for potential attackers (to be more vigilant) when she was alone. She also learned a few self-defense moves that would put John Cena to shame. (Just kidding, but we always tease her about it) Self-defense is as important for your confidence as it is for teaching you skills that can save your life.

Harnessing the Power of Safety Tech

If you are living alone, or you frequently have to walk or drive home from school or work, then you should embrace safety tech and apps.[69] They can make a huge difference in emergency situations. The following can be of aid:

- **Your Smartphone:** Whether you have an iPhone or Android phone, you can share your location with one or more people.
- **Noonlight:** This app is made for emergency situations. All you need to do is press down on the on-screen button if you need help. When you release your finger, the app waits for 10 seconds, then sends you a PIN number. If you enter the PIN, they know you're safe. If

---

[69] Giordano, 2022.

you do not, they call the authorities and share your location.

- **Strava:** If you enjoy going out for a run, consider installing this app. It will share your location with friends and record your routes. Its safety feature is called "Beacon." It lets authorized friends know what time you started your activity, how long you've been active, and how much battery life you have left. You can ask your friends to check in on you at a specific time, so they can share your GPS map with authorities if required.

- **Rescu:** This app enables you to obtain help at four chosen residences. This can help save time if you need the police, fire department, or ambulance to visit you asap. You can send help to these addresses even if you aren't home. A typical scenario where this might be useful is if someone sees a robber breaking into your home while you are away. The sooner the police get there, the less likely the thieves are to get away with your treasured possessions.

1. How can a smart doorbell help keep you safe?
    a. It has a camera so you can see who is at the door.
    b. It rings loudly.
    c. It has various ringtones.
2. What is the median age at which young adults move away from home?
    a. 22
    b. 19
    c. 25

3. Fire escapes and exit doors should be:
   a. Unlocked
   b. Locked
   c. Transparent
4. What is an important sign that a home is safe?
   a. It is on the first floor or at ground level.
   b. All the windows and doors can be securely locked.
   c. Fire professionals can easily climb into a window via trees or shrubs.
5. What is one great app for emergencies?
   a. Strada
   b. Moonlight
   c. Noonlight

I hope this chapter has made you feel more confident about moving out on your own. Living alone can be a little lonely. Moving out with other students or any other safe person, on the other hand, can provide you with companionship, help in emergency situations, and a lending hand when you are not feeling at your best. Now that you have your living situation sorted out, let's get to another important decision that many teens have to make: choosing the right college and/or finding their first job.

Test Answers:
   1. a
   2. b
   3. a
   4. b
   5. c

Chapter Nine: Choosing a College and/or Finding Your First Job

"The path you choose to follow through life is yours and yours alone. When you look back at the steps you've taken, don't do so to try to see where you should have gone. Instead, just look how far you've come."

–Doe Zantamata

Deciding what you want to do with your life can be daunting when you are a teen. Some people seem to have a professional "calling" from a very young age. Others don't find their passion until they are older. Many continue to discover new areas of interest later in their adulthood. The good news is that there's always time to change. Choosing a course or profession isn't always a linear process.

A True Story: Life can take many twists and turns, and my best friend Nigel is testimony to this fact! He started out studying law, only to switch to psychology. After a few years in practice, he realized his passion lay in medicine and obtained a medical degree, specializing in gynecology and obstetrics. He now works as an obstetrician and heads a team at a big hospital.

Choosing a College

There are many more things to consider other than prestige when it comes to picking a college. These include:

- **Distance and Transportation:** You may think that travelling by bus or train for half an hour or longer is nothing, but commuting gets old really quickly and driving and even public transport can be super expensive! You should calculate how much you would spend to travel to and from college every day. It might be worth paying higher rent to live closer to your college.

- **Monthly Costs:** Most college websites give you a rundown of total costs, including fees, living expenses, and tuition. If you have to move away from home, include food, discretionary expenses, and rent. Average expenses in current times can be more or less as follows: [70]

  o **Room and Board:** You will need to spend around $13,620 to board at a private college, $11,950 at a public college.
  o **Books and Supplies:** Expect to pay round $1.240 per year.
  o **Transportation, Clothing, and Entertainment:** The cost for these can range from $2,870 to $3,400.
  o **Tuition fees:** The average tuition and fees at ranked colleges are as follows:[71]
    - $38,185 for private colleges
    - $22,698 for public, out-of-state colleges
    - $10,338 for public, in-state colleges
  o **The Length of the Course:** If you will be taking out a student loan, then every year you are at college counts immensely. This is because the longer your course is, the bigger your debt is

---

[70] College Data, n.d.
[71] Powell, Kerr, et al., 2021.

likely to be. Once again, it is a matter of crunching numbers. A degree with a big demand after you graduate may be worth the extra year or two.

Prices can vary from year to year, so the best way to determine real costs is to visit the individual website of the colleges you are considering. Most provide guides to living expenses and include information on everything from rent to book and supply costs.

- **Clubs and Other Social Opportunities:** One of the most exciting things about college is having the chance (and the time) to join a host of extra-curricular clubs where you can meet people, do the things you love, and be entertained. If you are torn between two colleges, check out what each offers in terms of extracurricular activities. Just a few educational institutions with great ratings in this respect include the University of Texas at Austin; the University of Michigan, Ann Arbor; the University of California, Los Angeles; and the University of Illinois at Urbana-Champaign.[72]

  The University of Texas at Austin, for instance, has more student organizations than any other college in the south. It also spends more than any other college in the US on athletics. The University of Illinois at Urbana-Champaign, meanwhile, was named the number one college for fun by *Business Insider*.

- **The School Calendar:** You will obviously have to adapt any personal plans you have to your school calendar, but it is worthwhile knowing that calendars can vary significantly from college to college. If you are interested in a specific summer job, or you have an important event

---

[72] Best Value Schools, 2020.

like a wedding coming up, therefore, be aware of potential incompatibilities.

- **The Availability of Mental Health Care Services:** I have mentioned that your first year of college is fun, but it can also be a little stressful because you have to adapt to so many changes at once. Most campuses have services like crisis intervention (such as hotlines) for students with urgent mental health issues. They also connect students to community resources and counseling services.

- **Mission Statements:** Feeling at home in your chosen college can be considerably easier if you are in a place whose educational philosophies you agree with. Your chosen college should speak to your values and inspire you to tread the path that will take you to your adulthood.

Useful Statistics:

- Around four in ten high school students say that cost is the most important consideration when they are choosing a college.

- Both parents and children often underestimate the actual costs of college. A 2021 survey by Fidelity Investments showed that 38% of high school students and a quarter of all parents believe that the total cost of attending college is a maximum of $5,000 a year.

Useful Tip: The price colleges indicate on their websites are only "sticker prices." For instance, Princeton University published a sticker price of almost $54,000 for tuition and fees in 2020-2021. However, the average amounts paid by students after accounting for needs-based grants was only $23,572. This just goes to show that it is very important to do your research, find out what grants are available, and aim to get a scholarship by getting excellent grades when you are still in high school.

Mental Health Fact: Colleges have seen a big spike in the number of students who have depression and who seek mental health services. Despite this fact, colleges have a widely varied record when it comes to responding to students' needs. Some institutions have gotten into a bit of a legal pickle because they have encouraged students with depression to take leave from college, instead of proving the help they need to deal with their mental health issues.

If you have anxiety and depression, it is especially important to find out what counselling and other mental health services are offered at your list of potential colleges. Find out how many counselling professionals there are on staff. Some colleges offer mental health services but have long waiting lists because they are understaffed. It may not be fun to read, but this is the plain truth: A recent national survey has shown that around 40% of college students experienced depression, one in three had anxiety, and one in seven said that they had experienced suicidal thoughts.[73] If you need help, get it. Build a network of friends that can help you when you need a lending hand or a friendly ear. Maintain your friendships and family relationships from back home, using Skype, Facebook, Snapchat, and other apps to stay connected.

Working Out Student Loans

If you plan on taking out a federal student loan, it is vital to understand that you may need several years to pay off the loan amount plus the interest.

The US Department of Education recommends students not borrow more than 8% of their projected gross income (the total income from all sources, including returns, discounts, and allowances, before deducting any expenses or taxes) or 20% of their "discretionary income" (the income remaining after deduction of taxes, social security charges, and basic living costs).

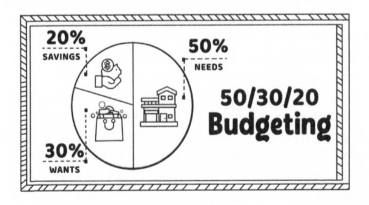

---

[73] Aslanian & Roth, 2021.

You may have heard of the 50/30/20 rule. It is a starting point that some financial planners use to develop budgets. It states that:

- 50% of your income should go towards fixed needs (like rent, insurance, healthcare, car payments, and minimum loan payments.
- 30% should go towards wants or variable expenses (clothes, dining out, etc.).
- 20% should cover savings and debt (emergency savings and additional debt payments).

However, for larger debts like your student loan (The average college debt among student loan borrowers in America is $32,731), a more realistic breakdown might be 60%/20%/20%, with:

- 60% of your income should go to fixed needs (including your monthly student loan payment and credit card payment).
- 20% should be reserved for savings and debt. If you are already saving 15% in your 401(k), put this 20% toward emergency savings, college savings, and extra debt payments.
- 20% remains for discretionary spending.

Question Time: What Is a 401(k) Plan?
When you start working, you will be offered a 401(k) plan, which gives you a tax break on the money you contribute. You can consider 401K as an employer-sponsored retirement plan. Your contribution is automatically taken from your employee paycheck and invested in your chosen fund. You, the employee, can match part or all of that contribution if you wish. There is a

maximum contribution limit of $20,500 in 2022 (or $27,000 for those aged 50 or older).

Paying Back Your College Loan

Find out the starting salary that people in your chosen profession earn. Calculate if this amount will be enough to afford your student loan using an online loan calculator like *Calculator Soup*. You can also visit Student Aid's *Loan Simulator*,[74] which helps you find the best student loan repayment strategy, change your repayment plan if you are struggling with payments, and explore the possibilities and effects of borrowing more money.

> **Useful Tip:** When paying back your loans, remember to prioritize those carrying a high interest rate (including credit card loans, which usually have a much higher rate than student loans).

Working While Studying

If you are a college student and time permits, having a part-time job is an excellent way to reduce the amount you need to borrow and to get your foot in the door of the workforce. You can find jobs in food service, but you should check out if there are on-campus positions available as well.

Jobs to consider include:

- library associate
- tutor
- teaching assistance

---

[74] Federal Student Aid, n.d.

- campus tour guide
- retail assistant
- freelance writer
- paid internships

Most paid internships take place during the summer. Although a summer job may interfere with plans of going back home, it can be worthwhile, especially if you are able to land a job in a company you would like to work for in the future. You can also earn enough money to sustain you throughout the year. Glassdoor reports that some internships pay as much as $8,800 per month.[75]

Finding Your First Job

If you would like to take a sabbatical or you do not intend on going to college, try to look for jobs in the areas that suit your skills and interests. Start by checking out sites that focus on teen job opportunities (like Snagajob.com). You should also consult popular job sites like Indeed and Monster. Finally, look through Help Wanted ads in the newspaper and the Employment Services job listings.[76]

> **Useful Tip:** Employers in industries like retail and hospitality are usually interested in hiring younger employees and providing the training required.

---

[75] Coursera, 2022.
[76] Doyle, 2021.

Writing a Professional-Looking Resume

When you're looking for a job, it is important to have a well-designed, professional-looking resume or CV and an online profile on LinkedIn. Don't worry if your resume is a little short. Employers will know that you are young, and they may be interested in "soft skills" (such as teamwork, organization, time management) rather than experience. You may not have worked professionally before, but you will undoubtedly have volunteered, taken part in team activities, completed one or more internships, and managed a complex schedule.

What Elements Should Your Resume Contain?

Prioritize the following features when writing your Resume:

- **A Standard Format Template:**[77] Most jobseekers use free resume templates, which are available in abundance online. To start off, use the reverse-chronological resume format. This lists your work experiences and education from most recent to oldest. This order of information makes sense because as you start working in more jobs, most human resources professionals will be most interested in what you are currently doing (or what you have recently done).
- **A Professional-Looking Font:** This is not the time for Comic Sans to take center stage. Instead, opt for classic fonts like Arial, Calibri, Tahoma, Times New Roman, or Lucida Sans.
- **A Practical Division of Information:** Instead of using a single-column layout, use two columns. It will allow you to fit more information on one page.
- **Useful Contact Information:** You can provide your phone number and email, but you should also offer your

---

[77] Career Blog, 2022.

LinkedIn URL. Make sure the information on your LinkedIn page matches what you write in your resume.

- **Your Objective:** For instance, you might write, "I am interested in putting my social media marketing skills to use by creating and uploading all social media content for a successful fashion firm." Make your objective short but sweet. Bear in mind that recruiters spend no more than seven seconds to get a first impression of you from your resume.
- **Detailed Education Information:** State the name of your college, your GPA, the courses you completed, the clubs you joined, and any other information that shows that you are a flexible, committed team player who can help a company achieve its goals.
- **Hard and Soft Skills:** Hard skills include the ability to use Excel. Soft skills include critical thinking, having a strong work ethic, problem-solving, and decision-making.

> **Handy Tip:** Keep your resume/CV to just one page unless you have over a decade or two of experience.

Acing Your Job Interview

Job interviews these days are often skills-based. This means that your interviewer will not ask you generic questions about your "strong" and "weak" points but rather, request that you mention specific examples in which you displayed a skill that is necessary for the job. To provide good answers, you need to study the job description well and understand what skills are required to succeed. You also need to have specific instances in mind that demonstrate these skills. Recruiters may ask questions like, "Tell me about a specific time that you showed that you were a good team player." "Tell me about a time you missed a deadline and what you did about it," or "Tell me how you resolved a conflict at work." You should perform role plays with friends and family members so you feel comfortable and have many prepared example answers.

1. How much do books and school supplies cost annually?
    a. Around $1,240
    b. $5,000
    c. $15,000
2. What is a college's "sticker price?"
    a. The price advertised on a college's website and brochures
    b. The amount paid by scholarships
    c. The price listed on a college's website minus scholarships, grants, and financial aid
3. The US Department of Education recommends that you borrow no more than what percentage of your projected gross income?
    a. 8%
    b. 10%
    c. 12%
4. What is the 60%/20%/20%?
    a. A way to pay back your mortgage
    b. A way to make the most of your investments
    c. An ideal breakdown of how you should spend and save your earnings

5. What is a 401(k) plan?
    a. A plan to buy a home
    b. A contribution taken from your employee paycheck that is invested in a fund of your choosing
    c. An amount that goes into your savings account

Now that you've got all the practical considerations out of the way (including student loans, finding a home, and health insurance), it's time to work on something many people don't identify as one of the biggest challenges teens can face: the complex world of emotions.

Test Answers:

1. a
2. a
3. a
4. c
5. b

Chapter Ten: Overcoming Emotional Challenges

"When you react, you let others control you. When you respond, you are in control."

–Bohdi Sanders

As you transition into adulthood and living independently, you can face many emotional challenges such as depression, loneliness, and stress. You are certainly not the only one going through this. You may find that your emotional states are more volatile, and it is hard to stay calm in tense situations. In this chapter, I will share strategies for regulating your emotions and feeling more positive about the road that lies ahead.

Statistics Time: Anxiety and depression are common among college students, with 41% of students experiencing anxiety and 36% battling depression, as found by the Association for University and College Counseling Center Directors.[78] However, just being a teenager in and of itself involves facing various issues, the most pressing of which I will identify and help you overcome.

The Emotional Challenges Faced by Teens

If you feel that the quality of your life would suffer if you didn't have a smartphone or desktop computer, I'm not here to argue with you. I sometimes feel like my mouse and keyboard are

---

[78] American Psychological Association, 2013.

extensions of myself. I am dependent on them for work, and they are also the means through which I interact and network with friends and people who share my interests. I'm mad about tech, and when it comes to spending on wants, I would pick a great laptop computer over a pair of off-white sneakers any day. However, I often remind myself to exercise moderation and to embrace other activities that force me to get off my desk (or the comfort of my couch). Below are just a few factors that are increasing stress in teens.

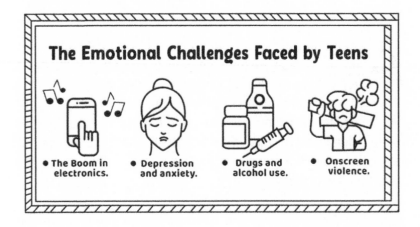

The Emotional Challenges Faced by Teens

- The Boom in electronics.
- Depression and anxiety.
- Drugs and alcohol use.
- Onscreen violence.

The Boom in Electronics

Despite being a self-confessed tech geek, I cannot deny that electronic media has dramatically changed the way we form and build relationships. Social media and other online facilities may have many upsides, but they can also cause damage if they aren't used with moderation. It's not so bad for older generations like mine, since we started out in the tech game late. Research has shown, however, that because technology is so prevalent in the lives of young people, it can affect their interpersonal skills. For instance, they can find it hard to pick up on social cues or body language, because much of their communication is via messaging, chats, and similar.

> **Tip:** Try to create a rich social life that blends the very best of technology and in-person bonding. Organize sports days, beach clean-ups, or meals together with friends. I can assure you that nothing beats seeing your best friend break into laughter!

Depression and Anxiety

Around 13% of teens can experience depression before adulthood and nearly one in three teens will experience anxiety at some point.[79] What is causing this phenomenon? Below are just a few reasons:

- The pressure to do well at school, be great at sports, and have many friends or be popular is common amongst teens.
- Many are scared by the increase of recent attacks.
- Comparing oneself to others on social media is something we all deal with.

> **Tip:** If you think you might have anxiety or depression, talk to your parents about it. You might be surprised to learn that one or more parents may have had (or still have) similar struggles, and they may have handy advice to give you.

---

[79] Morin, 2020.

If your anxiety or depression is strong, seeing a therapist is advisable. They can suggest very useful therapies that can help you feel much better, sometimes in a short time frame. One approach that is very popular and that is all-natural, is cognitive-behavioral therapy. This is aimed at pointing out the vital links between how you think, feel, and behave. The therapist may recommend that you try out a new behavior when you are in a situation that provokes stress and then jot down the way it affects how you feel or think about this situation. They can also help you reframe negative thought patterns into healthier ones.

I have spoken about social media in Chapter Two, and I suggested setting limits for how much screen time you should enjoy daily. Doing so will not only help you sleep better but also help you feel better about yourself. If you love science and research, you will find that countless studies link excessive social media use to mental health problems. It's not about being radical but rather about finding balance.

Drug and Alcohol Use

It's a tough subject, but I don't want to shirk away from it, and neither should you, because it is something you will most probably come across in your teen years. Teens can find it harder to control impulses, and they are also subject to more peer pressure than adults. Therefore, they can find it hard to decline alcohol or substances when these are offered to them by peers.

Tip: When I was 21 and studying in college, I remember that a few people in my group of friends used to drink, and a couple would smoke marijuana when we would go out. I declined because I was always worried about how these substances could affect my memory when I was older. Moreover, I was a runner, and I always liked to feel energetic and at my best during a morning run in the park. I know it can be hard to say no when you want to fit in, but it really is all about confidence. If you are yourself and you accept others but make your own decisions regarding your own body and health, your friends will respect you. Nobody ever made fun of me or insisted when I said no, and anyone who does these things is probably not a very good friend.

On-Screen Violence

Watching violent movies, TV shows, or video games desensitizes teens, dulls their emotional responses to aggression, and has the potential to promote aggressive behavior, as found in a 2010 study.[80] While it is difficult to avoid aggressive images altogether, it is important to differentiate right from wrong and fantasy from reality. Try to consume media with your parents and have an honest chat about things you deem inappropriate, fantastical, or exaggerated. Be on the lookout for issues such as sexism and other inappropriate treatment of human beings and other sentient beings like animals.

I have named just a few challenges you may be facing, but I have mentioned many more throughout this book. Other issues that can make you feel less happy, peaceful, or confident include obesity, academic issues, and bullying.

Setting Healthy Boundaries

Drug and alcohol use, peer pressure, and academic pressure often come from outside sources like friends and classmates.

---

[80] Strenziok, et al., 2010.

Whenever you feel pressured to take part in risky activities, say words, or engage in habits that may harm your physical and mental health, learn how to set healthy boundaries. In order to do so, You must become comfortable enough to say "no."

If someone proposes an activity you don't want to be involved in, don't give too many excuses or reasons when you decline the invitation. Use "I don't" instead of "I can't" language. Confidently say, "Sorry, I don't smoke," "I don't drink," "I don't lend my books," or "I don't approve of bullying."

Know that friends may try to influence you and initially laugh or criticize you if you don't bend to their will. If you have always said "yes" to them in the past, they will probably try to make you change back to how you used to be. Stick to your guns, without losing your cool. In time, they will respect you and learn that if they want to remain in your life, they will have to respect your boundaries.

A Friendly Tip: Know that your teenage years aren't the "be-all, end-all" of your life. It may seem like your whole life will end if you don't get straight As or if you aren't the most popular kid in class, but it actually won't. Even if you don't get into your dream college course, you can always pick up credits in community college and eventually make the shift. Reward yourself for effort—not only for good results.

Black Swans

These are just a few celebrities who were generous and honest enough to admit that they had a tough time in high school:

- **Charlize Theron:** The Atomic Blonde actor, who won an Oscar for Best Actress in *Monster*, spoke about having been bullied at school.
- **Selena Gomez:** She may be one of the hottest names in music and beauty, but Selena described herself as a nerd who "would have been destroyed" if her cousin had not been head of the cheerleading team.
- **Ryan Reynolds**: He says that at school he was a pariah who didn't know how to talk to girls. Things have certainly changed for the comedic actor, who is now one of Hollywood's biggest heartthrobs.

There are many examples of people who blossomed into beautiful swans in their adult years. Remember that every day is a new chance to reinvent yourself, change your style game, try a new activity, and pick up skills that will help you communicate better with others.

Speaking to Your Parents or a Trusted Adult

If you are being bullied or pressured or you are depressed, tell your parents or a trusted adult about it. If they suggest going to a therapist, see it as a boon! So many fantastic and super successful people see a therapist as a way to identify and talk about problems and identify ways to be happier. There are many successful approaches you can try when you're feeling a little low. I mentioned cognitive-behavioral therapy, but there are others that can help in so many ways. Some people who have anxiety, for instance, find great comfort in taking part in theater, dance, or music making activities. Others feel that art therapy is an ideal way to express emotions they find difficulty putting into words.

Battling College or Work Stress

You may find that many things you relied on others to help you with (including waking up on time, getting to class or work, and timing study for exams) are suddenly your responsibility exclusively. Leaving home can be stressful from an emotional perspective, in that you may not have your parents, siblings, and best friends right next to you, ready to pick you up when you're feeling down. Similar stressors can occur when you begin college and/or start working in a new job. To battle college stress, make sure to:

- **Make nutrition, exercise, and good sleep a priority.** Follow the nutrition tips from Chapter Two and make sure to sleep at the same time every day and avoid technological distractions in the hours before bedtime.
- **Try pet therapy.** Research has shown that pets reduce stress. One study by University of British Columbia researchers found that therapy sessions for stressed-out college students are growing in popularity at many

colleges in the US. [81] This is because the results they produce are no less than remarkable. In the study, students who simply spent time cuddling and playing with dogs in a therapy session showed significant reductions in stress and boosts in happiness and energy. They felt these positive effects even 10 hours after their session was over.

Many people in the US, UK, and many other parts of the world have emotional support pets. These pets do not receive specific training, but they can help with many conditions, including:

- anxiety
- depression
- learning disabilities
- ADHD
- chronic stress
- and more[82]

- **Rely on your college's mental health services.** Drexel University has a Recreation Center with a mental health kiosk. There, students get a "check-up from the neck-up" for free and receive information regarding mental health resources and supports.[83] Find out what is available on different campuses before making your choice of which college to attend.

A True Story: Claire used to get panic attacks while studying for her college entrance exams. She told me about how bad it was getting, and one day, she felt so anxious that she actually agreed to join me for a yoga class! She loved it, and the teacher

---

[81] Ward-Griffin et al., 2018.
[82] Alvarado Parkway Institute, n.d.
[83] Eva, 2019.

suggested that she should sign up for a yoga and mindfulness meditation stress course when Claire told her about her struggles. Claire was able to control her stress before it gave way to panic, and now, she always completes controlled breathing exercises before important exams.

Test time!

1. Can emotional support pets help with depression?
2. What is cognitive-behavioral therapy?
3. Can watching a lot of violent media make you aggressive?
4. Should you use the word *don't* or *can't* when you want to say no?
5. How many teens experience anxiety at some point in their lives?

Your teen years may have their share of emotional challenges, but they are also a time in which you make some of the best friends and memories you will ever have. If you want to learn how to get on with others and communicate effectively, move along to the next chapter.

Test Answers:
1. Yes. Even though they do not receive formal training, these dogs can help with many mental health conditions.
2. It is a therapy that seeks to help you understand the important connection between how you think, feel, and behave. It can help with various issues—including anxiety and depression.
3. It can potentially increase your aggression, yes.
4. Don't doubt it. Use the word *don't*!
5. 13%

Chapter Eleven: Building Healthy Relationships with Others

"The most basic of all human needs is the need to understand and be understood."

–Ralph Nichols

I f you sometimes feel like it's hard to describe what you're feeling or control the way you express yourself when you're angry, know that these emotions are very common among people your age. Numerous scientific studies have shown that there are powerful reasons why it may be harder to communicate with others assertively, control your anger, or be in a good mood all the time when you are in your teen years. These changes and challenges aren't permanent, and by being aware of them, you can start managing them productively and building healthy relationships with others.

Emotional Challenges for Teens

In your teen years, you go through numerous changes that can make it harder to communicate with others. These can include:

Hormonal Changes

In your teen years, hormones like estrogen, progesterone, and testosterone (the sex hormones) fluctuate. These hormonal swings can cause mood shifts and make it harder to control your impulses and emotions.[84]

---

[84] Newport Academy, 2012.

> **Fun fact:** Being impulsive isn't all-bad. In fact, scientists have found that teens are more impulsive and sensation-seeking because impulsivity plays a key role in evolution. It allows you to learn crucial information about the environment.[85]

Risk-Taking

Taking risks is sometimes given a bad rap by the media, but it can be positive, negative, or both, and it can have negative and/or positive outcomes. Taking risks is all about exploring. When you move outside your comfort zone, you can discover new things about yourself and the world around you.

For instance, you may know you're good at swimming, but you might decide to take a risk and try out something new and exciting like scuba diving (with trained professionals). Beneath the surface of the ocean, you may find that you suddenly fall in love with marine life, and your experiences may lead you to think about studying Marine Biology when you're older.

You might decide to take up the guitar, sign up for a cooking class, or accept your classmate's invitation to go see a movie together. This might introduce you to new people with whom you will one day launch a start-up. You never know where life will take you, but if you are too safe and your life always follows predictable routines, you can miss out on many interesting opportunities.

---

85 Constantinidis & Luna, 2019.

When risks take place in a supportive, supervised, and positive environment, they can lead to many gains. However, sometimes teens take risks because of peer pressure, because they underestimate the real risk of a situation, or because they have not taken time to weigh the pros and cons of behaving in a specific way.[86] When in doubt, speak to your parents or a trusted adult about decisions you are thinking of making. Choose someone who listens to you and doesn't judge you but is capable of pointing out insights that you may not have considered. This mentor will be able to lead you on a safer (but still fun) path.

Loneliness and a Sense of Disconnection

A 2021 study published in the *Journal of Adolescence*[87] has shown that there have been global increases in teen loneliness, with twice as many teens feeling lonelier than they did ten years ago. Approximately 40% of people aged 16 to 24 said that they felt lonely "often" or "very often."

Question Time—Why are Teens Lonelier?
There are many reasons why it can be hard to connect with others when you are going through such immense change. The parts of your brain that regulate emotions are still maturing, so the emotional effects of loneliness can be stronger.

Teens additionally may not have mastered the art of making the most of "me time." Therefore, when they are left alone, they may feel bored or simply not know how to fill up their free time meaningfully.

Some may have social anxiety, which is an intense fear of being judged or watched by others. Don't worry; this is often all

---

[86] University of Minnesota Extension, n.d.
[87] Twenge et al., 2021.

transitory. Little by little (and by taking "reasoned risks") you can try new things out, sign up for clubs, try new sports and activities, and do many more things that will make you feel like part of something greater than yourself!

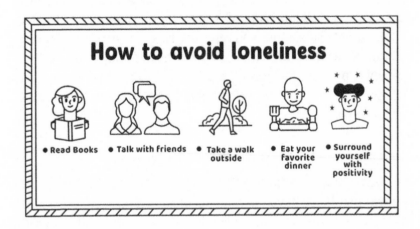

Difficulties Concentrating

A study published in the *Journal of Neuroscience* has shown that teens who find it hard to concentrate or feel confused may be hapless victims of neurobiology.[88] Using MRI scans, researchers monitored the brain activity of teens while they were trying to complete a task and ignore distractions. The scans revealed a somewhat chaotic level of activity in the prefrontal cortex, which is involved in making decisions and multitasking.

This activity occurs because teens have too much gray matter. As teens age, the amount of gray matter their brain has decreases, and it becomes easier to focus. Difficulties with concentration are not only relevant to school and grades. They can also make it harder to connect with others because in order

---

[88] Hill, 2010.

to really get to know people, it is important to listen to what they are saying and make sure they know we are doing so.

Teens can also sometimes find it hard to explain what they are thinking when they experience overwhelming emotional input. This occurs because the connections between the emotional and decision-making parts of the brain are still developing.

Don't let the knowledge of these changes make you feel helpless. You might find it harder to focus than an older person, but that does not mean you can't do so when you put your mind to it. It just means you must be a little more aware of when you are distracted so you can bring your mind back to the present moment. Mindfulness meditation is a fantastic way to teach your mind to remain "in the here and now" instead of wandering.

Difficulties Reading Others' Emotions

A study published in the *Journal of Nonverbal Behavior*[89] has found that teens are far less able to accurately read the range of emotions in the voices of other teens. This is particularly true when it comes to reading emotions like anger, happiness, disgust, or meanness. Funny enough, teens are perfectly able to understand adults' tone of voice. Why the difference? The answer is that teens have not yet reached the maturity levels they need to identify or express vocal emotions. They find it easier to understand older adults because the latter are more experienced at expressing their emotions.

Honing Your Communication Skills

Being aware that there are vital changes taking place in your brain is a great place to start, but these changes do not mean that you can't create great relationships with others. To do so,

---

[89] Morningstar, M et al., 2018.

work on some of the most important skills that people of all ages need to interact with others socially and professionally. Read on to discover what these skills are!

Knowing and Regulating Your Emotions

It can be hard to control feelings like anger or frustration if you are not aware of how you feel before a "blow-up" occurs. There is a myriad of emotions you may be feeling, including anger, disappointment, excitement, loneliness, frustration, elation, happiness, tiredness, and more. All these emotions can affect how patient you are with others, how interested you are in listening to them, and how you deal with people who seem to be pushing your buttons.

In order to regulate your emotions and speak properly to others, you need to be emotionally aware. One way to hone this skill is keeping a journal to write down the highlights and low points of your day, trying to describe how they made you feel. After a few days, try to notice patterns. Answer questions like:

- What did I feel when "situation A" happened?
- What type of situations usually make me angry or uncomfortable?
- Why did what person A say to hurt me so much?
- Why do I think an argument took place with someone? Is there anything I might have said that furthered the tension? Is the other person undergoing difficulties, or is there any reason why they might have behaved that way?

Useful Tip: Be aware of physical cues that you may be tired, angry, or stressed! When you are waiting for an exam to start, you may find that your heart races or that you feel your ears or cheeks getting hot. When you are angry, you may notice a churning feeling in your stomach or a tightness in your chest. Your ears may feel hot, or your face may go red. By identifying these signs early, you can take steps to calm down. You might seek a little distance from the situation and practice a little controlled breathing or head to a green space to gather your thoughts.

Emotional awareness helps you feel more in control. Instead of just reacting emotionally to stimuli, you can use assertive verbal and body language to ensure your personal boundaries are respected.

Learning to Listen

It can be hard to control your impulse to interrupt others, but to make friends, being an active listener is key. Allow your friends the time they need to tell you how they are feeling or what they are thinking. Use body language to show you are listening. For instance, you can nod your head occasionally and try to mirror their facial expressions. Use words to reassure them you understand them. Try the following sentences to start off with:

- "I see."
- "That must have been tough."
- "I understand why you feel this way."
- "Of course."
- "Yes, that's logical."

You can also show your interest in what others say by asking them to tell you more about their thoughts, emotions, and experiences. Use questioning phrases like:

- "That sounds like fun. Tell me more about it."
- "What do you like most about football?"
- "Who is your favorite author? Why?"

Avoid questions with a "yes" or "no" answer, as these questions do not promote a continuous flow of conversation.

Speaking to Others Assertively

Learn to say "no" or state your point of view calmly but confidently. Use "I" instead of "you" language so that others do not feel attacked. Tell them how things make you feel instead of telling them what they are doing wrong.

Avoiding Triangles

If you are mad at friend A, don't tell friend B about it. Talking to one person about another can give rise to a "toxic triangle" that doesn't solve any problems. You don't have to fix things in the heat of the moment, but you should try to sort out problems with friends, letting them know if something upset you in a kind, gentle, yet confident manner. Focus on what you felt instead of on what they did so they don't feel defensive, and they will be more open to understanding you.

Focusing on Solutions

When a discussion arises with a friend, try to focus on the solution (where you want to head) instead of taking a blaming approach. Aim to see yourself and your friend as members of a team instead of opponents. See how each of you can compromise to achieve an outcome that is acceptable to both of you.

Knowing How to Start and End Conversations

Knowing how to start a conversation is a great way to make new friends and expand your social circle. Do you remember a time in which you initially thought someone was serious, too quiet, or arrogant, only to discover they were the total opposite when you got to know them better?

It's very hard to break stereotypes and counter first impressions if you never make an effort. Moreover, there may be someone you are interested in dating at a party that you would love to approach and get to know. The art of conversation isn't really a mysterious art at all; it simply involves using your body language and speech to indicate that you are friendly and interested in getting to know someone.

If you want to start a conversation with a person or join a group of people who are chatting together, first, observe what's going on. Do they look like they're in the midst of a serious discussion or like they are having a private laugh or even a brainstorming session about something personal? If so, it might not be the best time.

If, on the other hand, things seem casual and it seems like they wouldn't mind someone coming up to them, approach them casually. Do the same if you see someone alone, using a conversation starter such as:

- "Hi Tim, how's it going?
- "Hey, long time no see!"
- "So, what have you been up to lately?"
- "Hi, I'm Jude, your classmate from Criminal Law. How are you doing? What do you think of Professor Murray's class?"
- "That looks like a good book. What's it about?"

Knowing how to end a conversation is also important. You shouldn't stay longer than time permits, but you shouldn't end things abruptly or awkwardly. Try phrases like:

- "It was great chatting you. I gotta' go now but hope to catch up with you next time."
- "Time for my swimming class. Talk to you soon."

- "My class is starting now, but I hope to hear more about how your mom is doing next time. Take care."

True Story: My son Neil struggles a bit with starting conversations, but he has a friend, Jim, who is very confident. When they are at a new place, Jim goes up to people and says, "Hi, I'm Jim, nice to meet you." Neil said when Jim did this for the first time, Neil found it embarrassing. Imagine his surprise when he noticed that the people Jim had approached were delighted and started chatting with him. Neil decided to copy Jim and now goes up to others and introduces himself to them when he is at a party or social event. It has made him many new friends!

1. Why do teens sometimes find it hard to control their impulses?
2. Can you name one good way to start a conversation?
3. Can you name one sentence you might use to end a conversation?
4. How can you show someone that you are really listening to them?
5. Can you name one way to be more aware of your own emotions?

The teen years are filled with change and possibilities. Know that you can define a future filled with meaning and purpose. Your current abilities and interests do not define you; you always have room to grow, change, and advance. In the following chapter, I will encourage you to adopt a growth mindset. I will also make it easier for you to adopt two crucial skills: choosing healthy habits and making decisions.

Test Answers:

1. Their brain is still maturing, and they are undergoing many hormonal changes.
2. "Hi, guys, what have you been up to lately?"
3. "It's time for my basketball training, gotta go and train. It was great catching up. Hope to see you soon."
4. Nod and say phrases like, "I see," or "That must be tough."
5. Use a journal to observe the situations that make you feel happy, angry, sad, tense, and similar. Try to observe patterns in the way you behave in the face of challenging and pleasant moments.

Chapter Twelve: Embracing a Growth Mindset, Setting Goals, Adopting Good Habits, and Making Wise Decisions

"Once your mindset changes, everything on the outside will change along with it."

–Steve Maraboli

I n order to learn good habits and make smart decisions, it is important to face the challenges of life with a growth mindset. Stanford University professor, Carol Dweck, coined the term *growth mindset*, differentiating it from a "fixed" mindset. People with a growth mindset do not believe their innate talents and abilities are fixed. By working hard and committing to goals, people can excel at new activities, hobbies, and skills they may not have mastered in the past.

A Growth Mindset

Busting Myths

Dweck has found that people often mix up what a growth mindset is.[90] Below are just a few misconceptions about this concept you should get out of the way from the start.

1. **A pure growth mindset exists, and you already have it.** Even if you feel you are very positive or you are always open to growth and change, in reality, most people have a blend of fixed and growth mindsets. There is no such

---

[90] Dweck, 2016.

thing as a "100% growth mindset." Knowing this can help you approach developing a growth mindset as just another vital life skills you can learn, practice, and refine.

2. **A growth mindset only involves praising effort and hard work.** Dweck argues that it is useful to not only reward pure effort, but to do the same for learning and progress and to emphasize the processes that foster them. Beneficial processes can include asking others for help, trying out new strategies, and capitalizing on setbacks to progress effectively.

3. **Simply saying that you have a growth mindset will guarantee that you will achieve it.** To be real, and attainable, you have to "walk the walk," not just "talk the talk."

Examples

If you wondered what the difference between a growth and fixed mindset is, it can best be explained by giving practical examples of a fixed mindset vs a growth mindset. Below are just a few.

Difference between Fixed Mindset and Growth Mindset

Fixed Mindset	Growth Mindset
• "I've never been good at reading, so I could never finish The Lord of the Rings."	"I might try reading The Hobbit as the events take place before The Lord of the Rings and it has less pages to read. This way I can pick up information and expand my vocabulary, so I will feel more confident when I start The Lord of the Rings."
• "My boss at the cafe said the cappuccino I made for a customer lacked froth. She's always criticizing me. I can't stand this job!"	"When there is lull during my shift today, I will practice using the machine to make a killer cappucino froth."
• " I could never walk up to someone I dont know."	"Hey, there's the new kid from class. I might go up to them and ask how they're doing. Even if I find it hard to ask pertinent questions, I can let them know they can count on me if they need anything."

Tips for Developing a Growth Mindset

A growth mindset takes time to build and perfect, but you can start by following these tips:

- Avoid judgmental statements like "I'm not good at..." or "I could never do that..."
- See failure as a chance to work out a more productive strategy for next time.
- Do things to obtain the results you want—not to receive the approval of others.
- Find opportunities to celebrate the successes of others.
- Say "yes" to new experiences and chances to learn or challenge yourself.

Building Good Habits and Breaking Bad Ones

Setting a routine is an important way to manage your time well, reduce stress, and ensure all your goals are met. Embracing good habits involves more than following a schedule, of course. It requires you to commit to making positive choices that will enhance your knowledge base and promote better physical, mental, and even spiritual health.

Most people recommend that you should set goals if you want to adopt healthy habits that will lead you to success and happiness. However, James Clear, author of *Atomic Habits,*[91] has an interesting spin that I find to be very insightful. Clear argues that the secret to breaking bad habits and embracing useful ones, is to associate all you do with your identity.

---

[91] Clear, 2018.

Linking Fruitful Habits to Your Identity

Ask yourself questions that connect your activities with your identity, such as: "What type of person is well-liked?" You can answer this question with an answer like: "Maybe it's the type of person who accepts invitations and says yes to new activities."

You can also link habits to your identity by telling yourself things like, "I'm an investor," instead of "My aim is to invest around $200 and see how it does on the stock market." By connecting the act of investing to who you are, making money on stocks will seem less like a dream and more like something you can start achieving now.

Consider Good Habits to Have a Compound Effect

Do you remember in Chapter One, when I spoke about compound interest as a way to passively make money from money? Good habits are a bit like that. All the seemingly small things you do to achieve your goals have benefits whose added value you may perceive many years down the line.

Keep the Habits That Serve You, Drop Those That Don't

Human beings pick up habits because our brains identify a way of behaving as the solution to the many challenges we face. However, you should aim to sit back and identify which habits are helping you feel healthier, happier, and more successful, and which are harming you or simply keeping you in a rut.

Clear Your Surroundings of Distractions

If you are studying for a big exam, isn't it much easier to avoid falling into the temptation of checking Instagram every few seconds if you block this app temporarily or leave your phone in another room? Your distraction may be music, the television, or junk food. Identify the things that are steering you from your goal and try to eliminate them from your surroundings.

Manage Your Time Well

Use a diary to list all the things you have to do on a given day. Give yourself a reasonable time to achieve each of your goals. Cross out everything you have achieved and make sure to prioritize any important task you have not completed for the next day. To keep your mind on track, turn your phone off or place it on airplane mode, remove physical distractions such as your tablet or PlayStation from your workspace, and divide big goals into smaller ones. Reward yourself for achieving both mini-goals and major ones.

Embrace the Laws of Behavioral Change

Clear states that to form good habits, you should make your goal easy, attractive, satisfying, and evident (in other words, there should be cues in your environment that keep your goal in your mind). In order to break bad habits, try removing the cues that point you to distraction. Reframe them in your mind into things that are unattractive, difficult, and unsatisfying.

For instance, if you started an unhealthy habit like smoking and you want to stop, remove all cigarettes from your environment, read about the effects of cigarettes on your health, and write down how smoking makes you feel. It may leave you breathless, make it harder to work out, or result in an unpleasant cough. Use the money you used to spend on cigarettes for a gym membership or another fruitful activity.

Know Your Obstacles

If you have a habit you would love to adopt—like do more exercise—but you find that the days go by and, for some reason, you haven't started working out, try to identify your main obstacle. For instance, in the case of fitness goals that never get fulfilled, your main bugbear could be one of the following reasons:

1. You don't like working out in public.
2. You don't have the right workout gear.
3. You don't have the time to take public transport to the gym and back.

Write down as many real obstacles as you can and brainstorm at least three ways to deal with them. For instance, if you feel shy about exercising in front of other people, what about signing up for an online exercise streaming service or investing in a small treadmill and a set of free weights?

Learn How to Set Reasonable Goals

Teens are inherently go-getters, so if you have numerous plans and ambitions, way to go! A survey undertaken by teen blogging community, Stage of Life, revealed some fascinating statistics:[92]

- Approximately 74% of teens set goals for themselves, and around 92% of high school and college students said they were reaching for goals when surveyed.
- Around 81% of teens have failed to attain an important goal.
- Almost 42% of teens prioritize educational goals, followed by community, purchasing, and financial goals (in order of preference).
- Almost half of all teens use a journal or planner to keep on top of their goals.

---

[92] PR Web, 2013.

How Can Teens Benefit from Setting Goals?

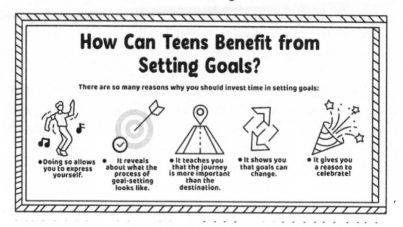

The goals you set should be personally fulfilling. However, they should also follow specific criteria to ensure they are achievable and worth the effort and time investment.[93] These criteria make up the mnemonic acronym S.M.A.R.T. The idea is that you should aim to set goals that are:

1. **Specific:** For instance, if your goal is to read more books during the year, set a specific number of books—like one book a month.
2. **Measurable:** Define what evidence will prove you are progressing and re-evaluate this evidence if necessary.
3. **Attainable:** Be reasonable; don't set goals that are impossible to achieve, as repeated failure will only make you feel unmotivated. In the book example above, don't set reading two books per week as your goal if you are too busy at school or work for this to be possible or if it will mean you can't carry out your usual activities like taking part in exercise, seeing friends, and similar.

---

[93] Lindberg, 2020.

4. **Relevant:** Your goals should be in accordance with your values and your long-term plans.
5. **Time-Based:** Assign a target date by which you can check if you have attained your goals.

Consider your target to be a general guide. In reality, you may need to change it as you go along. The important thing is to stick to a regular schedule. Taking a week or month longer to do so than you initially planned is usually okay if you are steadily working toward your goals.

Once you have decided the goals you wish to attain, work out a plan and list the steps you will take to accomplish them. Regularly reflect on your progress and consider changing up a few strategies if needed. Stay motivated by visualizing yourself achieving what you set out to do, making mood boards, and telling yourself positive things every day. You can tell yourself:

- "I am confident."
- "I am powerful."
- "All I need is within me at this moment."
- "I have the strength I need to give my best to my goal today."
- "I am making big improvements every day."

Finally, don't forget the power of teamwork and support. Ask for help when you need it and share your plans with friends and family so they can provide helpful advice or information. Remember to reward yourself as you complete the steps you need to achieve your goal.

Making Decisions

Teens have to make a host of decisions, ranging from what sports to take part in, to what subjects to specialize in when they are older. We have spoken of many of these decisions in previous chapters (such as choosing a college, deciding where to work, and selecting the goals you wish to save for). The following strategies can make your task easier:

- **Brainstorm your options.** Scribble a few on a piece of paper—even those that may sound absurd. Leave your journal and come back to it in a few hours. You may find that one of the ideas you didn't think much of, can produce a "lightbulb moment" that changes absolutely everything.

- **Write down the pros and cons of each option.** [94] This can be very useful for just about any conundrum in life, ranging from whether you should accept a job to whether you should start dating someone new. You will be surprised to see that you probably already know which decision has the most pros, but you need to muster the courage to make crucial changes.

- **Be true to your passions, likes, and (if you believe in it) your destiny.** Feeling very strongly about something is part and parcel of intuition. This "hunch" or "gut feeling" is actually a combination of past experiences and what is occurring in the present moment. It is the "inner voice" that can help you feel more confident about your decisions because it is a powerful reminder that you hold the ultimate power to make decisions that will impact your life. If you needed further convincing, take note. A 2016 study found that using non-conscious information (or intuition) can help people make better, more accurate decisions. [95]

- **Allow yourself to make mistakes.** Remember that so-called "failures" are the greatest teachers you may

---

[94] Morin, 2021.
[95] Lufityanto et al., 2016.

encounter in life. When they occur, they can seem disastrous and monumental, but with the passage of time, you can think about them and strategize all the steps you can take to avoid them in the future.

- **Have a plan B... and C.** Have a few back-up plans in case the decision you make doesn't produce the result you wanted.
- **Be self-compassionate.** Being self-compassionate is very simple. It involves being as kind to yourself as you would to others. One 2018 study published in the journal *PLOS ONE* showed that self-compassion can protect you from the harmful effects of perfectionism.[96] If you tend to be self-critical, find ways to be kind to yourself daily. Take an energizing walk in the woods, meet someone you love for a meal out, or get your hair styled. Embrace all the tiny things that can bring a bounce to your step.

True Story: Claire grew up never taking a dance class because someone once laughed at her during a school choreography. One summer, she signed up for Zumba class at the local gym, thinking it was just an aerobics class. She was surprised to find it was all about raising your heart rate through one of the activities she most loved as a child—dance! Today, she still attends Zumba classes and parties and feels much more confident about moving her body to lively beats!

---

[96] Ferrari et al., 2018.

Test time!

1. Why can making mistakes be positive?
2. What is a positive affirmation?
3. What is the growth mindset?
4. What does the acronym S.M.A.R.T. stand for?
5. What is self-compassion?

I hope I have inspired you to set goals, adopt good habits, and make strategic decisions but also to see failure as one of the most powerful ways to learn, reframe your thinking, and grow as a student, friend, family member, and person.

Test Answers:

1. Mistakes can be great teachers, and they can help us strategize so that our outcomes are better next time.
2. A positive affirmation is something you can say to yourself daily so you feel more motivated.
3. The growth mindset is a way of seeing yourself as able to grow, learn, and pick up new skills.
4. S.M.A.R.T. is a strategy for goal setting. The letters indicate your goals should be specific, measurable, attainable, relevant, and time-based.
5. Self-compassion involves being kind and non-judgmental with yourself.

Conclusion

"Enjoy the journey and try to get better every day. And don't lose the passion and love for what you do."

–Nadia Comaneci

Throughout this book, I have shared numerous life tips that I hope will give you a confidence boost when you are ready to begin your life as a young adult. If I could sum up all the knowledge I gained along so many years of being a child, teen, and then an adult and mom, I would repeat the words of world-famous gymnast, Nadia Comaneci: "Enjoy the journey."

When you're a teen, it somehow seems that the world's biggest "winners" are a bit older than you. Your idol might be a successful YouTuber like KSI, a singer like Rosalia, or a footballer like Cristiano Ronaldo. If so, read up a little about their lives. You may find that in their teen years, they were probably very much like you. Some famous adults (like Cristiano Ronaldo) overcame great poverty and other challenges, working hard to prove they could exceed expectations and eventually became shining examples of commitment, talent, and effort.

Every single tech billionaire, software developer, or singer probably went through a stage of confusion when they didn't know what they were meant to do, and many took a long time to find their passion. All learned from their mistakes. One example is multi-award-winning-singer, The Weeknd (Abel Makkonen). He underwent periods of homelessness and went through a troublesome phase which, he says, encouraged him "to smarten up, to focus." He is the perfect example of the growth mindset at work.

Your actions are separate from your identity, and you are always better than your worst action. This does not mean you shouldn't strive to be better. Quite the contrary; I want these words to give you hope. Every day is a new day in which to find your passion, make a healthy change to your diet or exercise routine, and embrace organization and tidiness in your living space.

Aside from making you feel hopeful about your adult years, I have also given you many practical tips you can use as a guide when you are in a pickle. Imagine you drive over a nail and the "flat tire" signal pops up on your dashboard. There's no need to panic. Just drive to a safe spot, pull this guide out, and calmly follow the steps I have provided.

I have tried to cover most areas that are relevant to teens and young adult life—including honing your financial literacy, leading a healthy lifestyle, and managing your own medical matters when you move away from home. Read my book from start to finish, because I have provided important tips, such as getting your personal medical records ready before (not after) you leave home. By having relevant documentation at hand, you can easily find a new doctor and keep them updated on your medical history.

I have also shared my favorite family recipes—all of which take less than 15 minutes to prepare and can be put together in a flash to throw a dinner party for your friends. Of course, you are more likely to feel better about inviting people home if your abode is neat and tidy. Having a well-organized, attractive home says a lot about the type of person you are and where you are heading.

Fashion is equally important. Even if you aren't a mini-John Galliano or Stella McCartney or you don't have thousands to spend on a new wardrobe, a few basics will set you on the right track. Knowing how to shop is essential as well. It is better to spend more on quality items that won't go out of style, than splurge on a pair of Jordans, only to find that you don't have a good suit in your wardrobe when you are invited to a formal event.

My book additionally covers the first independent steps you will take as a young adult, including driving a car, moving home, choosing a college, or finding your first job.

To succeed in college or your workplace, it is essential to sharpen your emotional intelligence. I have, therefore, delved into the importance of identifying and regulating your emotions, communicating well with others, knowing how to listen, and resolving conflicts assertively but kindly.

I ended my book by talking about the extent to which healthy habits and wise decision-making can keep you focused on your goals and help reduce stress. Approach new people and experiences with a growth mindset. Know that you were not born with a fixed or limited set of talents and abilities. Your biggest passion may be something you have yet to discover.

If I could add one last piece of advice, it would be to be kind to yourself. Embrace your mistakes with self-compassion and humor and see what you can learn from them. Negotiate relationships with gentleness and a commitment to finding solutions to problems instead of lingering on past hurt. Your teen years are a uniquely beautiful time in your life—one filled with growth, change, and so much potential. Your journey has just begun!

If you enjoyed my book, I would love it if you could leave a positive review on Amazon. I self-publish my books, so I don't have a big marketing company I can rely on to spread the word about me. I would love for more teens to read my book so they can feel a little more confident as they cross the bridge from their teen years into young adulthood. If you can help make it happen, that would be amazing!

THANKS FOR READING MY BOOK!

I sincerely hope you enjoyed this book, and that you will benefit from implementing the Life Skills discussed.

I would be incredibly grateful if you could take a few seconds to leave me an honest review or a star-rating on Amazon. (A star-rating only takes a couple of clicks).

Your review helps other young adults discover this book, and may also help them on their life journey. It will also be good Karma for you.

Scan this code to leave a review.

IF YOU FIND THIS BOOK HELPFUL, YOU MIGHT ALSO LOVE:

Here's what others are saying about Vivian:

 Kclark649

★★★★★ **Loved it!!**
Reviewed in the United States on August 25, 2022
Verified Purchase

It's absolutely a great read. I love to learn especially when it comes to my kids, learn how to be a better parent a listening parent snd this book breaks down everything you will need to hear on how to do that.

 Milas Barber

★★★★★ **Worth Reading. Very Practical**
Reviewed in the United Kingdom on March 31, 2022
Verified Purchase

I hope every parent will get a chance to read the book since it provides helpful and practical tips to keep calm in heated situations. It advises us how to be a happier/healthier parent and raise happy confident children so that you provide a safe place for them. It reminds us that the children need to feel loved and respected. Easy Reading with great advice!

Scan this code to check-out Vivian's other books.

SOMETHING FOR YOU!

Get your printable workbook today!

Scan this code to download.

References

AA. (n.d.). *Feeling flat? Here's how to use jump leads.* https://www.theaa.com/breakdown-cover/advice/using-jump-leads

Active health. (n.d.). *What are the negative side effects of too much screen time?* https://www.activehealth.sg/read/screen-time/what-are-the-negative-side-effects-of-too-much-screen-time

After Market News. (2019, January 3). *Cooper tires survey shows 81 percent of Americans have had a flat tire and 74 percent say they know how to change a flat tire.* https://www.aftermarketnews.com/how-many-americans-know-how-to-change-a-tire/#:~:text=Cooper%20Tires%20survey%20shows%2081,to%20change%20a%20flat%20tire.

Agero Insights. (2019, November 19). *Vehicle breakdowns cost US economy $41B per year.* https://blog.agero.com/vehicle-breakdowns-cost-us-economy-41b-per-year

Alvarado Parkway Institute. (n.d.). *How emotional support animals benefit mental health and wellness.* https://apibhs.com/2020/05/18/how-emotional-support-animals-benefit-mental-health-and-wellness#:~:text=Some%20common%20mental%20disabilities%20that,and%20post%2Dtraumatic%20stress%20disorder.

American Psychological Association. (2013). *College students' mental health is a growing concern, survey finds.* https://www.apa.org/monitor/2013/06/college-students

Anderson, M., & Jiang, J. (2018, May 13). *Teens, social media and technology 2018.* Pew Research Center.

https://www.pewresearch.org/internet/2018/05/31/teens
-social-media-technology-2018/

Ariel. (n.d.). *Washing symbols explained.*
https://www.ariel.co.uk/en-gb/how-to-wash/how-to-do-
laundry/fabric-care-labels

Aslanian, S. & Roth, A. (2021, August 19). *Under pressure:
Inside the college mental health crisis.* APM Reports.
https://www.apmreports.org/episode/2021/08/19/under-
pressure-the-college-mental-health-crisis

Atlanta Parent. (2021, March 15). *Best money and budgeting
apps for kids.* https://www.atlantaparent.com/best-
money-and-budgeting-apps-for-kids/

Bathroom City. (n.d.). *Germs in your bathroom: Everything you
need to know.*
https://www.bathroomcity.co.uk/blog/germs-your-
bathroom-everything-you-need-
know#:~:text=There%20are%20around%20200%20milli
on,sink%20and%20insides%20of%20showers.

Bennet, J. (2014, August 6). *Majority of teens say they don't
know how to change a tire.* The Wall Street Journal.
https://www.wsj.com/articles/majority-of-teens-say-
they-dont-know-how-to-change-a-tire-1409025661

Berger, R. (2022, May 8). *5 apps to help teens start investing.*
Forbes.
https://www.forbes.com/sites/robertberger/2022/05/08/
5-apps-to-help-teens-start-
investing/?sh=49783ce75c9e

Best Value Schools. (2020, August 11). *Colleges with the best
extracurriculars.*
https://www.bestvalueschools.com/rankings/colleges-
extracurricular-activities/

Boys & Girls Clubs of America. (2022, January 19). *The
importance of goal-setting for teens.*
https://www.bgca.org/news-stories/2022/January/the-
importance-of-goal-setting-for-

teens#:~:text=The%20Importance%20of%20Goal%2DSe
tting%20for%20Teens&text=Teenage%20goal%2Dsettin
g%20can%20help,work%20ethic%20and%20build%20p
erseverance.&text=Goals%20give%20us%20something
%20to,hard%20work%20%E2%80%93%20something%2
0to%20celebrate.

Brigs, S. (2018, October 23). *8 ways to build good habits and break bad ones*. Open Colleges. https://www.opencolleges.edu.au/informed/features/8-ways-build-good-habits-break-bad-ones/

Care Spot. (n.d.). *Finals season: Common illnesses for college students*. https://www.carespot.com/blog/common-illnesses-in-college/

Career Blog. (2022, January 4). *How to write your first job resume*. https://novoresume.com/career-blog/first-job-resume

Catana, K. (2022, June 18). *How much screen time is too much for teenagers? You might be surprised*. New Folks. https://www.newfolks.com/stages/average-screen-time-for-teens/

Centers for Disease Control and Prevention. (n.d.). *Childhood obesity facts*. https://www.cdc.gov/obesity/data/childhood.html#:~:text=For%20children%20and%20adolescents%20aged,14.7%20million%20children%20and%20adolescents

Centers for Disease Control and Prevention. (n.d.). *Physical activity guidelines for school-aged children and adolescents*. https://www.cdc.gov/healthyschools/physicalactivity/guidelines.htm#:~:text=The%20Physical%20Activity%20Guidelines%20for,to%2Dvigorous%20physical%20activity%20daily.

Centers for Disease Control and Prevention. (n.d.). *Sleep in middle and high school students*. https://www.cdc.gov/healthyschools/features/students-

sleep.htm#:~:text=The%20American%20Academy%20of
%20Sleep,10%20hours%20per%2024%20hours.

Clear, J. (2018). *Atomic habits: tiny changes, remarkable
results: an easy & proven way to build good habits &
break bad ones*. New York, New York: Avery, an
imprint of Penguin Random House.

College Data. (n.d.). *How much does college cost?*
https://www.collegedata.com/resources/pay-your-
way/whats-the-price-tag-for-a-college-
education#:~:text=For%20the%202021%2D2022%20aca
demic%20year%2C%20the%20average%20price%20of,
out%2Dof%2Dstate%20residents)

Constantinidis, C. & Luna, B. (2019, August 20). Neural
substrates of inhibitory control maturation in
adolescence. *Trends in Neurosciences, 42*(9), 604-316.
https://doi.org/10.1016/j.tins.2019.07.004

Consumer Financial Protection Bureau. (n.d.). *Teenagers and
savings*. https://www.consumerfinance.gov/consumer-
tools/money-as-you-grow/teen-young-adult/explore-
saving/#:~:text=%E2%80%9CA%20good%20rule%20of%
20thumb,directly%20into%20his%20savings%20accoun
t.

Coursera. (2022, May 26). *5 types of part-time jobs for college
students*. https://www.coursera.org/articles/part-time-
jobs-for-college-students

Coy, W. (2018, October 18). *How to find a safe place to live
off-campus: Tips for college students*. Realtor.
https://www.realtor.com/advice/rent/safe-place-to-live-
off-campus-college-students/

DMC. (n.d.). *How to introduce the concept of taxes to kids*.
https://www.dmca.bc.ca/how-introduce-concept-taxes-
kids

Downey, A. (2017, April 7). *Germ Alert: This is how many
germs are lurking in your bathroom, and you'll be
surprised at the dirtiest spot*. The Sun.

https://www.thesun.co.uk/living/3272186/this-is-how-many-germs-are-lurking-in-your-bathroom-and-youll-be-horrified-at-the-dirtiest-spot/

Doyle, A. (2021, March 14). *Job search tips and advice for teens.* The Balance Careers. https://www.thebalancecareers.com/tips-for-finding-a-job-for-teens-2058651

Drive Safely. (n.d.). *10 steps to changing a flat tire.* https://www.drive-safely.net/changing-flat-tires/

Duffy, J. (2019, October 23). The body-clock science behind later school start times. BBC. https://www.bbc.com/worklife/article/20191023-the-body-clock-science-behind-later-school-start-times

Dweck, C. (2016, January 13). *What having a "growth mindset" actually means.* Harvard Business Review. https://hbr.org/2016/01/what-having-a-growth-mindset-actually-means

Equifax. (n.d.) *What is a good credit score?* https://www.equifax.com/personal/education/credit/score/what-is-a-good-credit-score/#:~:text=Although%20ranges%20vary%20depending%20on,and%20up%20are%20considered%20excellent.

Eva, A. L. (2019, January 11). *How colleges today are supporting student mental health.* Greater Good Magazine. https://greatergood.berkeley.edu/article/item/how_colleges_today_are_supporting_student_mental_health

Fashion Week Online. (n.d.). *15 must-haves for your college wardrobe.* https://fashionweekonline.com/15-must-haves-for-your-college-wardrobe

Federal Student Aid. (n.d.). *See your federal student loan repayment options with Loan Simulator.* https://studentaid.gov/loan-simulator/

Fernando, J. (2022, July 7). *What are index funds?* Investopedia. https://www.investopedia.com/terms/i/indexfund.asp

Ferrari M., Yap, K., Scott, N., Einstein, D. A., & Ciarrochi, J. (2018, February 21). Self-compassion moderates the perfectionism and depression link in both adolescence and adulthood. *PLOS ONE, 13*(2). https://doi.org/10.1371/journal.pone.0192022

Finances Online. (n.d.). *47 essential student housing statistics you must learn: 2021/2022 data & demographics.* https://financesonline.com/student-housing-statistics/

Flatley, K. (n.d.). *How to teach kids to do their laundry independently.* Self-Sufficient Kids. https://selfsufficientkids.com/how-to-do-laundry-kids-teens/

Freedom Sprout. (n.d.). *15 money words your children need to understand.* https://freedomsprout.com/finance-terms-for-children/

Gerholdt, J. (2017, June 2). *4 companies embracing, and finding value in, the circular economy.* U.S Chamber of Commerce Foundation. https://www.uschamberfoundation.org/blog/post/4-companies-embracing-and-finding-value-circular-economy

Gibbons, S. (2018, June 19). *You have seven seconds to make a first impression: Here's how to succeed.* Forbes. https://www.forbes.com/sites/serenitygibbons/2018/06/19/you-have-7-seconds-to-make-a-first-impression-heres-how-to-succeed/?sh=23135e5456c2

Giordano, M. (2022, February 20). *The best personal safety devices, apps and alarms.* Wired. https://www.wired.com/story/best-personal-safety-tech/

Good Year. (n.d.). How to measure tire tread depth. https://www.goodyear.com/en-US/learn/tire-basics/how-to-measure-tire-tread-

depth#:~:text=Insert%20a%20penny%20into%20your,ti
me%20to%20replace%20your%20tires.

Healthy Options. (2018, July 14). *Kids' health: Tips for buying
and preparing fresh produce.*
https://www.healthyoptions.com.ph/articles/kids-health-
tips-buying-and-preparing-fresh-
produce#:~:text=Choose%20produce%20that%20is%20
not,and%20lettuce%20in%20the%20refrigerator

Hill, A. (2o10, June 1). *Why teenagers can't concentrate?* The
Hindu. https://www.thehindu.com/sci-
tech/science/Why-teenagers-cant-
concentrate/article16240168.ece

Hutton, J., Dudley, J., Horowitz-Kraus, T., & DeWitt, T. (2019,
November 4). Associations between screen-based
media use and brain white matter integrity in
preschool-aged children. *JAMA Pediatrics, 174*(1).
https://doi.org/10.1001/jamapediatrics.2019.3869

Iowa State University. (2014, March 31). *Limiting screen time
improves sleep, academics and behavior, ISU study
finds.*
https://www.news.iastate.edu/news/2014/03/31/parental
monitoring

John Hopkins Medicine. (n.d.). *7 heart benefits of exercise.*
https://www.hopkinsmedicine.org/health/wellness-and-
prevention/7-heart-benefits-of-
exercise#:~:text=Johns%20Hopkins%20research%20ha
s%20shown,impaired%2C%20leads%20to%20excessive
%20blood

Keebler, J. (2019, April 9). *How to replace a broken headlight.*
Car and Driver.
https://www.caranddriver.com/features/a27034088/how
-to-change-headlight/

Kids Health. (n.d.). *Strength training.*
https://kidshealth.org/en/teens/strength-

training.html#:~:text=If%20you%20are%20new%20to,w
eight%20or%20low%2Dresistance%20bands.

Lee, J. (2017, November 24). On Black Friday, the psychology
of retail rage. PBS.
https://www.pbs.org/newshour/science/why-black-
friday-leads-shoppers-to-behave-
bonkers#:~:text=The%20term%20%E2%80%9CBlack%2
0Friday%E2%80%9D%20first,become%20profitable%20
for%20the%20year.

Lindberg, S. (2020, November 26). *Tips for goal setting:
Helpful suggestions for self-improvement.* Verywell
Mind. https://www.verywellmind.com/tips-for-goal-
setting-self-improvement-4688587

Live Strong. (n.d.). *The max heart rate during exercise for
teenage boys.*
https://www.livestrong.com/article/369376-the-max-
heart-rate-during-exercise-for-teenage-boys/

Lonch, E. (2022, April 8). *This is why Americans can't manage
their own money.* CNBC.
https://www.cnbc.com/video/2022/04/08/financial-
literacy-in-
america.html#:~:text=Only%2057%25%20of%20adults%
20in,CNBC%20%2B%20Acorns%20and%20Momentive%
20survey

Lufityanto, G., Donkin, C., & Pearson, J. (2016, April 6).
Measuring intuition: Nonconscious emotional
information boosts decision accuracy and confidence.
Psychological Science, 27(5), 622-634.
https://doi.org/10.1177/0956797616629403

Mayo Clinic. (n.d.). *Mediterranean diet for heart health.*
https://www.mayoclinic.org/healthy-lifestyle/nutrition-
and-healthy-eating/in-depth/mediterranean-diet/art-
20047801

Mayo Clinic. (n.d.). *Tween and teen health.*
https://www.mayoclinic.org/healthy-lifestyle/tween-and-

teen-health/in-depth/teens-and-social-media-use/art-
20474437#:~:text=Another%202019%20study%20of%2
0more,and%20depression%20or%20anxiety%20sympto
ms.

McDonough, L. S. & Picard, C. (2019, March 22). *The ultimate
cleaning schedule for your day, week, month, and year.*
Good Housekeeping.
https://www.goodhousekeeping.com/home/cleaning/a3
7462/how-often-you-should-clean-everything/

McMarthy, C. (n.d.). *Anxiety in teens is rising: What's going
on?* Healthy Children.
https://www.healthychildren.org/English/health-
issues/conditions/emotional-problems/Pages/Anxiety-
Disorders.aspx

Meredith, G. R., Rakow, D. A., Eldermire, E. R. B., Madsen, C.
G., Shelley, S. P., & Sachs, N. A. (2020, January 14).
Minimum time dose in nature to positively impact the
mental health of college-aged students, and how to
measure it: A scoping review. *Frontiers in Psychology,
10.* https://doi.org/10.3389/fpsyg.2019.02942

Milken Institute. (2021). *Financial literacy in the United States.*
https://milkeninstitute.org/sites/default/files/2021-
08/Financial%20Literacy%20in%20the%20United%20Sta
tes.pdf

Minyanville. (2021, December 14). *Risk tolerance: Financial
risk tolerance.* Intuit Mint Life.
https://mint.intuit.com/blog/investments/investing-101-
risk-tolerance/#7

Morin, A. (2020, June 24). *Top 10 social issues teens struggle
with today.* Verywell Family.
https://www.verywellfamily.com/startling-facts-about-
todays-teenagers-2608914

Morin, A. (2021, January 13). *Steps to good decision-making
skills for teens.* Verywell Family.

https://www.verywellfamily.com/steps-to-good-decision-making-skills-for-teens-2609104

Morningstar, M., Ly, V. Y., Feldman, L., Dirks, M. A. (2018, January 16). *Journal of Nonverbal Behavior, 42*, 237-251. https://doi.org/10.1007/s10919-018-0274-7

My Home by Freddie Mac. (2022, February 7). *3 benefits to sharing your living space.* https://myhome.freddiemac.com/blog/rental-housing/3-benefits-sharing-your-living-space

Newport Academy. (2012, December 15). *Teenage hormones and sexuality.* https://www.newportacademy.com/resources/empoweri ng-teens/teenage-hormones-and-sexuality/#:~:text=Teen%20hormones%20affect%20teen agers'%20moods,think%20about%20dating%20and%20 sex.

Parra M. (2021, May 11). *How to fill air in a car's tires.* Wiki How. https://www.wikihow.life/Fill-Air-in-a-Car%27s-Tires

Participation. (2018, March 1). *How much screen time is too much for teens?* https://www.participaction.com/en-ca/blog/how-much-screen-time-is-too-much-for-teens#:~:text=The%20recommendation%3A%20Accordi ng%20to%20the,%2C%20Instagram%2C%20Snapchat% 20and%20YouTube.

Perina, K. (2014, February 27). *Gray matters: Too much screen time damages the brain.* Psychology Today. https://www.psychologytoday.com/us/blog/mental-wealth/201402/gray-matters-too-much-screen-time-damages-the-brain#:~:text=Even%20kids%20with%20a%20%E2%80% 9Cregular,position%20on%20screen%20time%20manag ement.

Powell, F., Kerr, E., & Wood, S. (2021, September 13). *See the average college tuition in 2021-2022.* U.S. News.

https://www.usnews.com/education/best-colleges/paying-for-college/articles/paying-for-college-infographic

PR Web. (2013, October 31). *Teen statistics about goal setting released by StageofLife.com.* https://www.prweb.com/releases/teens/goal-setting/prweb11288739.htm#:~:text=%2D%2D75.4%25%20of%20teenagers%20set,currently%20working%20on%20a%20goal.

Red Star Education. (n.d.). *The effects of financial illiteracy.* https://www.redstareducation.co.uk/blog/the-effects-of-financial-illiteracy/

Ro, C. (2020, March 11). *Fashion accounts for around 10% of greenhouse gas emissions from human activity, but there are ways to reduce the impact your wardrobe has on the climate.* BBC. https://www.bbc.com/future/article/20200310-sustainable-fashion-how-to-buy-clothes-good-for-the-climate

Sleep Foundation. (2022, March 11). *How to determine poor sleep quality.* https://www.sleepfoundation.org/sleep-hygiene/how-to-determine-poor-quality-sleep

Strenziok, M., Krueger, F., Deshpande, G., Lenroot, R. K., van der Meer, E., & Grafman, J. (2010, October 7). Fronto-parietal regulation of media violence exposure in adolescents: a multi-method study. *Social Cognitive and Affective Neuroscience, 6*(5), 537-547. https://doi.org/10.1093/scan/nsq079

SWNS Digital. (2021, October 4). *81% of recent college grads wish they were taught more life skills before graduation.* https://swnsdigital.com/us/2021/07/eighty-one-percent-of-recent-college-graduates-wish-they-were-taught-more-life-skills-before-graduating/

Teen Toolkit. (2017, March 21). *How to iron clothes.* https://www.teentoolkit.net/blog/how-to-iron-clothes

Teens Health. (n.d.). *Health insurance basics.* https://kidshealth.org/en/teens/insurance.html#:~:text=I n%20the%20United%20States%2C%20kids,COBRA

Teens Health. (n.d.). *Your medical records.* https://kidshealth.org/en/teens/medical-records.html#:~:text=If%20you%27re%20younger%20th an,who%20can%20see%20medical%20records

TNN. (2017, November 6). *Tips to buy the right meat.* Times of India. https://timesofindia.indiatimes.com/life-style/health-fitness/diet/tips-to-buy-the-right-meat/articleshow/9881702.cms

Twenge, J. M., Haidt, J., Blake, A. B., McAllister, C., Lemon, H., & Le Roy, A. (2021, June). Worldwide increases in adolescent loneliness. *Journal of Adolescence, 93*(1), 257-269. https://doi.org/10.1016/j.adolescence.2021.06.006

Tyrell, R. L., Townshend, T. G., Adamson, A. J., & Lake, A. A. (2015, March 11). 'I'm not trusted in the kitchen': Food environments and food behaviours of young people attending school and college. *Journal of Public Health, 38*(2), 289-299. https://doi.org/10.1093/pubmed/fdv030

U.S. Bureau of Labor Statistics. (n.d.). *Independence for young millennials: moving out and boomeranging back.* https://www.bls.gov/opub/mlr/2014/article/independenc e-for-young-millennials-moving-out-and-boomeranging-back.htm#:~:text=The%20median%20age%20at%20the, (See%20figure%201.)&text=Table%201%20shows%20t hat%20the,out%20than%20Blacks%20or%20Latinos.

U.S. Department of Agriculture. (n.d.). *Food waste FAQs.* https://www.usda.gov/foodwaste/faqs#:~:text=How%20 much%20food%20waste%20is,percent%20of%20the%2 0food%20supply.

U.S. Food & Drug Administration. (n.d.). *7 tips for cleaning fruits, vegetables.*

https://www.fda.gov/consumers/consumer-updates/7-tips-cleaning-fruits-vegetables#:~:text=Gently%20rub%20produce%20while%20holding,bacteria%20that%20may%20be%20present.

U.S. Securities and Exchange Commission. (n.d.). *Mutual funds.* https://www.investor.gov/introduction-investing/investing-basics/investment-products/mutual-funds-and-exchange-traded-1

United States Environmental Protection Agency. (n.d.). *Why indoor air quality is important to schools.* https://www.epa.gov/iaq-schools/why-indoor-air-quality-important-schools#:~:text=EPA%20studies%20of%20human%20exposure,times%20%E2%80%94%20higher%20than%20outdoor%20levels.&text=These%20levels%20of%20indoor%20air,percent%20of%20their%20time%20indoors.

University of Minnesota Extension. (n.d.). *Teens and risk-taking.* https://extension.umn.edu/teen-development/teens-and-risk-taking#:~:text=Parents%20often%20think%20of%20risky,well%20as%20when%20and%20where.

Unlock Food. *How to store vegetables to keep them fresh.* https://www.unlockfood.ca/en/Articles/Cooking-Food-Preparation/How-to-store-vegetables-to-keep-them-fresh.aspx#:~:text=Most%20vegetables%2C%20like%20carrots%2C%20potatoes,of%20the%20fridge%20than%20fruit.

Vallverdú-Queralt, A., Jáuregui, O., Medina-Remón, A., & Lamuela-Raventós, R. M. (2012, March 2). Evaluation of a method to characterize the phenolic profile of organic and conventional tomatoes. *Journal of Agricultural and Food Chemistry, 60*(13), 3373-3380. https://doi.org/10.1021/jf204702f

VIB. (2019, February 4). *A gut feeling for mental health.* https://vib.be/news/gut-feeling-mental-health

Viilagrasa Blasco, B., García-Jiménez, J., Bodoano, I., & Gutiérrez-Rojas, L. (2020, August 12). Obesity and depression: Its prevalence and influence as a prognostic factor: a systematic review. *Psychiatry Investigation, 17*(8), 715-724.

Ward-Griffin, E., Klaiber, P., Collins, H. K., Owens, R. L., Coren, S., & Chen, F. S. (2018, March 12). *Stress & Health, 34*(3), 468-473. https://doi.org/10.1002/smi.2804

Wells Fargo. (n.d.). *How to check your credit score and report.* https://www.wellsfargo.com/financial-education/credit-management/check-credit-score/#:~:text=How%20to%20check%20your%20credit%20score%20and%20report

Made in the USA
Las Vegas, NV
03 January 2023

64856493R00111